THE MORAL DIMENSIONS OF TEACHING

THE **MORAL DIMENSIONS**
OF **TEACHING**

Language, Power, and Culture
in Classroom Interaction

CARY A. BUZZELLI
BILL JOHNSTON

NEW YORK   LONDON
ROUTLEDGEFALMER

Published in 2002 by

RoutledgeFalmer
29 West 35th Street
New York, NY 10001

Published in Great Britain by

RoutledgeFalmer
11 New Fetter Lane
London EC4P 4EE

RoutledgeFalmer is an imprint of the Taylor & Francis
Group.

Printed on acid-free, 250-year life paper.
Manufactured in the United States of America.

    10 9   8   7   6   5   4   3   2   1

Library of Congress Cataloging-in-Publication Data is
available from the Library of Congress

ISBN 0-8153-3927-5

For Kasia; and for Ania, Piotrek, and Helen
—Bill Johnston

For Janice, my moral compass,
and for Andrew and Charles,
who help me see what is important in life
—Cary A. Buzzelli

CONTENTS

ONE

Introduction

The one thing needful is that we recognize that moral principles are real in the same sense in which other forces are real; that they are inherent in community life, and in the working structure of the individual. . . . The teacher who operates in this faith will find every subject, every method of instruction, every incident of school life pregnant with moral possibility.

—Dewey, 1909/1975, p. 58

This book is about the moral dimensions of classroom interaction. We will argue that many aspects of classroom interaction carry moral meaning, even though this meaning may not be apparent at first glance. We will support our argument by analyzing transcripts from a variety of classrooms to reveal the levels of moral meaning that can be seen in them. And we will offer a set of conceptual tools that can help teachers and observers of teaching to talk about the moral in classroom interaction.

As we will discuss, other researchers have analyzed the moral dimensions of what happens in classrooms. The present book extends this analysis in two ways. First, we will

1

show that a richer and deeper understanding can be obtained by looking at three features of classroom interaction: *language*, *power*, and *culture*. We will examine aspects of these three features to reveal moral meanings in classroom events.

Second, our analysis of the moral in teaching is informed with a sense of the moral complexities and ambiguities inherent in the practice of teaching. While not denying the existence of certain moral absolutes, we suggest that in most cases moral meanings constructed in classrooms are complex and multivalent. We thus eschew simplistic judgments about what is absolutely right and good in favor of an exploration of the moral layeredness of classroom interaction.

It is important as well to say at the outset what this book is not. As implied in the preceding paragraph, it is not prescriptive. We do believe in certain moral absolutes and will suggest that certain educational practices are preferable to others. But we believe the process of making morally right decisions is best left to the teacher. By the same token, we will not concern ourselves here with the "traditional" question of how moral decision making gets done, an issue that other researchers have examined in depth. This is an important line of research, but it is not our focus here. We are more concerned with sensitizing the reader to the often ambiguous moral meanings that inhere in actual classroom interaction. For us, then, a prime function of the book is to raise awareness of the usually hidden moral dimensions of schooling.

Finally, we wish to emphasize that although our focus is squarely on the classroom itself, we are well aware that the moral significance of education also resides in structures and practices beyond the classroom. There is moral meaning in all aspects of schooling, from national policy (one thinks of the standards movement, for example), through state and regional decision making, to schoolwide practices introduced by principals or sanctioned by tradition. Much of this has been effectively analyzed by other scholars. We acknowledge this work and, where appropriate, we will indicate the impact of broader moral forces on the classroom. Our focus, however, is the class-room itself and the moral meanings that are played out within it. This focus results in part from our firm belief that, whatever the influences on the teacher and the class from outside, the teacher still has the lead role to play in education, and a significant part of this role involves her work as moral agent.

To conclude this part of the introduction, it is crucial that we articulate our own understanding of what we mean by *morality* and *the moral*. We wish to emphasize that ours is not a technical or specialized understanding of morality. On the other hand, however, because these terms are widely used with somewhat different interpretations by many people connected with education, it is vital that we say as clearly and simply as we can what morality refers to in this book.

For us, morality constitutes that set of a person's beliefs and understandings which are evaluative in nature: that is, which distinguish, whether consciously or unconsciously, between what is right and wrong, good and bad. A moral judgment is one that adjudicates between, for example, a right and a wrong course of action. A moral issue is one in which some-one has to take a side based on considerations of what is right or good. A moral dilemma is a dilemma in which the options involve consequences that are both good and bad. Morality in this sense may involve judgments at a number of levels: It may refer to a person's behavior, or only to that person's thoughts, intentions, or words.

In an educational context, morality typically brings with it a certain set of concepts and ideas that are not often discussed in teaching and teacher education, being thought dangerous or inappropriate in schooling. These concepts include kind-ness, love, religion, spirituality, soul, and so on.

There are two other crucial qualities that distinguish the moral. First, much like knowledge of language, moral beliefs, values, and understandings are played out at the critical point of contact between the private, individual sphere and the social realm. Thus, moral beliefs are both "personal" and "cultural."

A crucial part of morality involves the interplay between these spheres. This quality reminds us that moral beliefs both vary from person to person and yet are also socially and culturally agreed upon. It also points to the profoundly moral character of relations between humans.

This dual nature of morality means that it is an open question whether morality involves fixed inner beliefs or is socially negotiated. We suggest that, in fact, both of these perspectives are valid. Moral beliefs tap into profound, personally felt values; yet they are also part of the social and cultural realms in which our understandings must be played out in language and other forms of interaction in order that they be clear, and which are influenced by relations of power and authority among the individuals involved. It is this very ambiguity that is the essence of the concept of morality, and why it has such an interest for us, especially in an educational setting: for it captures that encounter between the individual and the group that is in turn the quintessence of teaching and learning.

The same ambiguity is seen in the second major quality of the moral. At one level, moral values may be absolute. Yet at another, morality is contingent and contextually determined. The essence of morality lies partly in the dynamism between these two points. We hold what we think of as absolute values that are not influenced by circumstance; yet also, our view of what is right and good depends crucially on details of context. For us, the thing that we call *morality* is neither the absolute values nor the contingent values, but the dynamic interplay between them. In this, too, morality can be seen to exist at the meeting point of the private and the social.

Finally, we should clear up two potential misunderstandings and construct a couple of necessary conceptual fire walls. First, our use of the word *moral* has nothing in common with its use by the Moral Majority and other right-wing Christian organizations. Our understanding of what is right and good is not defined by a particular religious–political orientation. Second, we want to make an important distinction between morality and ethics. For the purposes of the present book, ethics refers primarily to codes of practice; thus, ethical values may be imposed on members of a profession (such as teaching) by the collective in the form of professional organizations and governmental bodies. Examples include the mandating of confidentiality in reporting grades or rules governing physical punishment. Morality, on the other hand, though it is usually played out in the social arena, also crucially involves personal, private values and beliefs. Thus, while it plays a central role in social activities such as teaching, it cannot be regulated by external institutions but must always be mediated by individuals.

THE ROOTS OF THIS BOOK

Our involvement in this project stems not just from our intellectual and academic interests but also from our personal experiences as teachers and teacher educators. As classroom teachers in diverse social and cultural contexts, we daily encountered dilemmas in the classroom. Working through these as best we could, we became aware, as all teachers do, of the countless moment-to-moment decisions that are involved in their resolution. Although some of these dilemmas were of a technical kind, many were what we would now describe as moral in nature: They involved issues such as how to be a good teacher to all students, how to strike a balance between kindness and firmness, and how to do well by the students when time and resources worked against us. In the years since we left classroom teaching for university teaching, we have revisited many of these dilemmas and over time have moved toward a fuller understanding of the broader issues that lay behind them.

Bill's Story

My thinking about morality in teaching sprang initially from a disillusionment with "scientific" ways of gaining knowledge about the educational process. As I began my doctoral studies a few years ago, I was excited about reading the huge literature on language learning and teaching that was made available to me. Yet ultimately I found myself disappointed by the findings presented in this literature. In an overwhelming majority of cases, comparisons of different teaching methods or approaches were inconclusive. Gradually, I came to realize that other, less tangible variables were at stake which experimentally designed science could not encompass and which were therefore ignored in the research literature: primarily, issues of relation.

Since, as it seemed to me, science could not ultimately offer a basis on which to make decisions about how to teach, I began to wonder how such decisions should be taken, and how they are actually taken in real situations. I came to a conviction that what guides us ultimately are moral beliefs, values, and standards: We select certain forms of materials, activities, and interactions because we believe that in a profound way, they are "for the best." This foundation is much harder to talk about than such notions as pedagogical effectiveness; but as I started to think at greater length and in more depth about the moral dimension of teaching, I had the feeling I was touching on the essence of teaching. This new way of conceptualizing classroom interaction, teacher–student relations, and teacher decision making helped me make sense of much that I had seen in my own teaching and that of colleagues and students, in ways that previous forms of research had been forced to ignore. It was this series of experiences that led me to write this book.

Cary's Story

Following my years as a teacher of young children and my doctoral studies, I began to examine how sociocultural theory, and Vygotsky's (1978) work in particular, might contribute to our understanding of moral development in children (Buzzelli,

1995, 1996). In this work, my focus was on the language used during dialogues about moral transgressions. As my research progressed, I began to reflect on my own experiences as a teacher of young children. I wondered how my conversations with the children had influenced their growth and development. I also wondered what moral implications my ways of interacting with my students had for me as a teacher and for the children under my tutelage.

These reflections caused me to return to a topic that was a keen interest of mine early in my graduate work—namely, the study of how language is used to create and convey meanings. My reading led me to consider how the semiotic or meaning-making function of language was a social experience and how it occurred within the context of a relationship with others. Further, the ways that meaning is created among individuals has tremendous significance for what those being initiated into the meanings come to learn and understand. It seemed that the social nature of such learning experiences also was laden with moral possibilities; that how we teach and what we teach have moral implications for ourselves and our students. Through my inquiry I came to see how those things I might not have originally thought of as moral were, in fact, "pregnant with moral possibility."

THE PRESENT PROJECT

In this book, we focus in particular on issues of language, of power and authority, and of culture in the process of exploring the moral significance of classroom interaction. In the educational literature, these three themes have played a central role over the last decade or two. Yet, surprisingly, through all the prolific discussion, their moral significance rarely crops up. The talk, rather, has been about how various modes of discourse create or limit learning opportunities and what comes to be labeled as knowledge; about the part played by power and authority in controlling students and regulating the knowledge discussed in class; and how issues of culture are either ignored or dealt with in unconsciously ethnocentric ways. We will argue that all these issues present teachers with predicaments that are moral in nature. Our task will be to fore-front the moral issues inherent in the problems of language, power, and culture in educational settings; to explore the nature of morality in these themes; and to offer a moral lens through which the themes, and the classroom dilemmas to which they give rise, can be viewed.

TEACHING AS A MORAL ACTIVITY

There is by now a long and well-established line of inquiry investigating the moral dimensions of teaching (Ayers, 1993; Jackson, Boostrom, & Hansen, 1993; Noblit & Dempsey, 1996; Noddings, 1984, 1992; Sockett, 1993; Tom, 1984). From their often different perspectives, these authors have all constructed an understanding of teaching as first and foremost a moral activity. It is this view of teaching which we share and which underlies the present book.

The existing literature on the morality of teaching has iden-tified two fundamental ways in which teaching is a moral activity: First, teaching is founded upon a relationship between two or more individuals. Second, teachers are engaged in changing the behavior of others to attain prescribed ends.

The first point reminds us that teaching is fundamentally relational, and that relations in turn are fundamentally moral in nature. Such an assumption underlies a lot of recent work in the morality of teaching. Noddings (1984), for instance, in her analysis of the caring relation, takes relation as "ontologically basic" (p. 3), prior to conceptions of the individual; she argues that relations are, in essence, moral. Furthermore, for Nod-dings, because morality is rooted in relation, and because rela-tions exist between specific individuals, morality is highly contextualized; moral judgments and decisions cannot be reduced to generalized rules, but must always be connected to, and recognize, "the uniqueness of human encounters" (p. 5).

The second point—that teaching involves changing people—has also been noted by a number of writers. Any educational endeavor includes the positing of certain goals and ends. These ends involve making decisions about what others should know and should become; such judgments, in turn, are based on questions of value and worth, making them moral judgments. In David Hansen's view, teaching as a practice "involves assisting students to broaden their horizons . . . helping students to become more knowledgeable rather than less so, more interested in learning and communicating rather than less so, and more expansive in the thinking in their human sympathies than less so" (1998, p. 649). Hansen goes on to note:

> Teaching embodies the human endeavor of moving human beings closer to the good, or, posed differently, closer to rather than farther from the prospect of a flourishing life. . . . Teaching constitutes an end in its own right, one infused with intellectual and moral promise. (p. 650)

Engaging with students to attain prescribed ends is the quintessential activity teachers undertake when they teach students, and it is through participation in the activity of teaching and learning that teachers and students alike create moral meanings. Thus, the claim Hansen is making and with which we concur is that rather than seeing, as some would, a need to ground the moral aspects of teaching in moral philosophy, moral theory, or other disciplines (e.g., Valli, 1990), the features that imbue teaching with moral significance are those features inherent in the practice itself. We feel this is a crucial point to make because many teachers and researchers have eschewed the examination of the moral dimensions of teaching for fear of becoming mired in arguments about moral philosophy and moral theory.

In this book, then, an underlying assumption will be that teaching is, above all else, a moral activity, because it is founded upon a relationship which involves making decisions and taking actions that influence the social, emotional, intellectual, and moral development of others in one's care. It is practiced within encounters between individuals in which one person seeks to assist and support the other in becoming a more knowledgeable, more able, and more thoughtful individual. Inevitably, this process relies on relationships in which a significant part is played by questions of moral values such as respect, dignity, and caring, and which require an acknowledgment of the uniqueness of both the learner and the teaching encounter. Working with others, in education and elsewhere, is intimate and demanding work that involves the constant play of moral values. If teaching is fundamentally moral in nature, it is also fraught with moral complexity and moral ambiguity. Indeed, it is precisely the features of teaching that make it a moral activity which also account for the complexity and ambiguity that teachers experience.

MORAL COMPLEXITY AND MORAL AMBIGUITY

Moral complexity and moral ambiguity are inherent, inevitable features of classroom life. It may even be that the ambiguity and complexity that surround moral issues account for the dearth of serious discussion about the moral aspects of teaching and learning in classrooms. Yet it would seem that vital questions need to be asked. How are moral complexity and moral ambiguity realized in classroom interaction? How can these features of classroom life be fruitfully discussed? And, above all, given this ambiguity and complexity, how is it that teachers know how to act in morally right and good ways?

Those of us who work in classrooms find ourselves as individuals and teachers constantly in situations of ambiguity, in moral predicaments that may be solved momentarily but whose final resolution lies beyond our grasp. Finding *the answer* that will simplify the complexity and clarify the ambiguity of teaching is simply not possible. Yet it was a quest that, not too long ago, was promulgated as possible. Indeed, "the moral thought and practice of modernity was animated by the belief in the possibility of a non-ambivalent . . . ethical code" (Bauman, 1993, p. 9). In other words, modern morality believed in and hoped to find "an ethics that is universal and 'objectively founded'" (1993, p. 10). This hope, however, has not come to fruition. What has become increasingly certain is that decisions whose consequences are unambiguously good tend to be of little existential importance. For Bauman, "the majority of moral choices are made between contradictory impulses" (1993, p. 11). This is a statement with which many teachers can readily identify, for they know that life in classrooms is, in Bauman's phrase, "shot through with uncertainty" (p. 11).

Bauman's comments echo the concerns raised by Burbules (1997). Burbules describes the tragic sense of education, by which he means the realization that, try as we might, as educators we can never be sure if things might have turned out differently. This realization calls us to consider, at once, both the opportunities and the constraints that inhere in our work as teachers. Teachers, then, are positioned at a "point of tension between seeing the necessity of things as they are and the persistent imagining of them turning out otherwise . . . of seeing at the same time the possibilities and the limits, the gains and the costs, the hopes and disappointments, of any human endeavor" (Burbules, 1997, p. 66). The tension between the possibilities and limits of teaching provides opportunities for teachers to learn anew from their disappointments and failures (e.g., the lesson that did not work), to examine their successes, and to reflect upon what has been gained by their students and themselves in the processes of teaching and learning. For Burbules, "the tragic sense" is not meant to be understood in a negative or pessimistic manner. Rather, it is meant to provide a "positive, constructive way to think about teaching and what it can and cannot accomplish" (Burbules, 1997, p. 66). Acceptance of our limitations should not cause us to limit our hopes; rather, it can be a source for continuing our efforts to care for and educate our students. The tragic sense of education, then, sets before us a number of moral challenges, our engagement with which is most visible in classroom interactions. And it is here, amid the moral complexities and moral ambiguities, that we will search for the moral meanings teachers and students create through their work together in classrooms.

THE MORAL NATURE OF CLASSROOM INTERACTION

We have argued that teaching is first and foremost a moral activity, and that the moral dimensions of teaching are inescapably complex and ambiguous. Because the focus of this book lies in an examination of the moral dimensions of classroom interaction, we must begin to identify particular features of classroom interaction that we can examine for their moral significance. What precisely is it about, and in, classrooms that can be called "moral"? Based upon the view of morality outlined above—namely, that it constitutes a person's beliefs and values about what is right and wrong or good and bad; that these beliefs and values are played out at the nexus of the personal and the social; and that, although there are moral absolutes, morality is also contingent and contextually determined—we believe that the following features of classroom interactions are at the core of the moral in classrooms.

The first morally significant feature of classroom interaction is that it involves teachers' personal and professional beliefs and values and the way they are enacted in the public setting of the classroom. Teachers continually make judgments about what to teach and how to teach, and such judgments involve deeply held beliefs and values that can be, and often are, distinct from those of other stakeholders in the educational process, such as principals and parents. These are judgments about what is valuable and worthwhile for children to know, do, and experience. These judgments involve, for instance, the selection of some experiences children will have rather than others, of engaging in some learning activities rather than others, of reading some texts rather than others, and of talking about some things rather than others. Granted, some teachers have less freedom and flexibility than others in their selection of curriculum and its implementation. To the extent that they are able to choose, however, their choices involve deliberations based upon their own values and beliefs, and a notion of what is best for a particular child or all the children in any given situation. There is, then, a prescriptive and normative nature to such decisions and choices that is guided by personal and professional beliefs and values (Clandinin & Connelly, 1995; Connelly & Clandinin, 1999).

There is a second way in which teachers' personal and professional values and beliefs imbue classroom interaction with moral significance. Classrooms are very complex places and, at times, the information available to teachers about some students is ambiguous at best. When teachers engage students in classroom interactions based upon personal and professional values and beliefs, they do so within a context of great complexity and, at times, great ambiguity. Both the complexity and ambiguity are due, in part, to not knowing exactly how decisions and actions will affect students. The acknowledgment that there are consequences for students, some of which can be anticipated in advance while others remain unknown, further highlights the moral significance of classroom interactions.

The second feature, then, concerns the ways teachers conduct themselves as they engage in constant moment-to-moment, day-to-day negotiations with students over innumerable issues and concerns. In the course of these negotiations, teachers and students must continually work through predicaments for which "once and for all" solutions will not be found. The constant need to seek solutions that are just, appropriate, and meaningful to the situation at hand calls for teachers to be attentive morally and intellectually (Hansen, 1998, 1999) to their students. Such attentiveness is demanding and requires a steadfast commitment to oneself as a teacher, to one's students, and to the acts of teaching and inquiry in which all are engaged. This is a moral commitment.

This leads to the third moral feature. The constant negotiation within oneself and with students concerning the enactment of teaching practices and curriculum must always be undertaken with a concern for how children are treated. To many educators and others who have spent even a short time in classrooms, this may seem obvious enough, as we are all aware of the importance of treating students with care and respect. However, recent examinations of classroom life (Burbules & Hansen, 1997; Hansen, 1999; Jackson et al., 1993) have brought into finer focus the many subtleties and nuances in the ways in which teachers and students interact with one another. The fleeting moments of a look, a facial expression, a response to a question, or an offhand comment all may carry moral meaning. Thus, in many different ways the relations created and enacted between teachers and students are a source of moral meaning for both and contribute to the sense each has of how they are being treated by the other.

Morality pervades many aspects of teaching and learning in classrooms. In the three features outlined above, however, the moral underpinnings of classroom interaction can be seen quite clearly to peek through the surface of classroom discourse. It is through classroom interactions that teachers and children create, maintain, and negotiate relationships as well as construct, acquire, and mediate the information that becomes shared, common knowledge (Edwards & Mercer, 1987). Yet, because the beliefs and values of teachers and students are involved as they engage in this creation and negotiation of relationships and knowledge, it is inevitable that classroom interactions are imbued with moral significance.

OVERVIEW

We have argued that teaching is a moral activity, that the moral dimensions of teaching are invariably and inevitably complex and ambiguous, and that the morality of teaching can be seen especially in certain aspects of classroom interaction. Our question now is this: How can we best talk about morality in teaching? Given these complexities and ambiguities, how might we approach the topic in a way that acknowledges these characteristics yet helps us to capture them in a manageable fashion?

Our response in this book is to examine morality in teaching through three lenses: language, power, and culture. We acknowledge that other frameworks and approaches are entirely possible in seeking to understand the moral dimension of teaching. Yet, for us, this tripartite framework has proved to offer valuable insights, and we will use it to structure the discussion here.

Why language, power, and culture? Our use of this framework is motivated by two principal lines of reasoning. First, these three areas represent some of the most important research and theory in the field of education in recent years. Work on language—for example, the analysis of classroom discourse—has revealed what Gordon Wells (1990) has called the "centrality of talk in education" and also the complexity of language use in classrooms, schools, and educational systems. The analysis of power in educational settings has led to the development of critical pedagogy and many other significant reconceptualizations of the macro- and micropolitics of teaching. A renewed interest in culture, in multiculturalism, and in hegemonies of cultural values has forced a radical reevaluation of representations of majority and minority cultures in education. This is not the place to set out these fields in detail; suffice it to say that, in each of the three areas, recent work has offered radically new and challenging reinterpretations of what does go on and what could and should go on in classrooms.

Our second reason for this focus is that, with very few exceptions, the otherwise admirable empirical and conceptual work on the morality of teaching conducted to date (and referred to above) has failed to examine in detail the moral significance of issues of language, power, and culture. Juxtapositions of morality with language, with power, and with culture have, by and large, not been made. Thus, the present project aims to extend that work by introducing concepts in the fields of language, power, and culture into the analysis of the moral significance of classroom interaction.

Let us point out that separating out issues of language, power, and culture for the individual chapters of the book is primarily an analytical convenience. We are well aware that in reality (i.e. in real situations, in classrooms and elsewhere) matters of language, power, and culture become inextricably intertwined. Language is used to negotiate or maintain power and is a primary vehicle for cultural productions; power is negotiated to a significant extent through language and in culturally conventionalized ways; culture is expressed largely through language; and hegemonies of culture are maintained by power. Thus, it is only temporarily, for the purposes of analysis, that we isolate these features of classroom interaction, acknowledging that in real life they interact in complex ways.

This said, the three central chapters of the book apply each of these three lenses in turn to examine the moral dimensions of classroom interaction.

In chapter 2, we look at the relationship between morality and language use in classroom settings. We consider the moral significance of a variety of forms of classroom discourse and how different forms of discourse serve to facilitate or hinder the nature and extent of students' participation in learning activities. Our purpose is to look at the ways different forms of discourse are used to establish and maintain the roles students play in learning activities, and thus what they learn and how they learn.

Chapter 3 takes up the theme of power in educational settings and its interrelation with moral values. We begin by arguing that, contrary to the claims of critical pedagogists and others, unequal power relations are an inherent feature of educational contexts. We go on to explore the notion of authority as the point at which power relations and moral meanings converge. In the body of the chapter, we look at three areas in which the moral significance of power relations in education is particularly clear: evaluation and assessment, including the moral dimension of examination practices; the control of bodies (that is, the ways in which teachers have the power to direct the physical business of schooling); and the ambiguities inherent in the notion of "empowerment" through voice and dialogue. We conclude by suggesting that any account of morality in teaching must acknowledge the foundational role of power relations in this domain.

In chapter 4, we take up the last of our three central themes: culture. Classrooms today include students from an ever-wider range of cultures, including those of established minorities; immigrant groups; indigenous peoples; and other ethnic, religious, and racial minorities. At the same time, "culture" is above all a set of values—of moral judgments. In this chapter, we examine encounters of different and sometimes incompatible cultures and cultural values in three areas: participation in classroom interaction; representation of nonmajority cultures in curricular materials; and identification, the process of claiming and assigning cultural and other identities in the domain of schooling. We conclude by suggesting that, in the interplay of moral meanings in actual classrooms, the three themes of language, power, and culture are always intertwined in inextricably complex ways.

In chapter 5, we consider the implications of our analyses in the preceding chapters for the practice of teaching and for teacher education and teacher development. We begin by arguing that a moral reading of classroom interaction and of teaching in general should lead teachers to nurture what we call the moral sensibilities: moral perception, moral imagination, moral reflection, and moral courage. We then consider how these *moral sensibilities* can be cultivated in the content and structures of formal teacher education programs, and also how they can underlie the processes of teacher development.

TWO

The Morality of Discourse

Examining the Language of Teaching and Learning

In language it is the combination of the experiential and the interpersonal that constitutes an act of meaning. All meaning—and hence all learning—is at once both action and reflection.

—Halliday, 1993, p. 101

Any Discourse is a *theory* about the world, the people in it, and the ways in which goods are or ought to be distributed among them . . . each of us has a moral obligation to reflect consciously on these theories . . . it is a moral matter and can change the world.

—Gee, 1996, p. 191

Briefly, all education is intrinsically a moral activity which articulates the dominant ideology(ies) of dominant group(s).

—Bernstein, 1990, p. 66

INTRODUCTION

In the previous chapter we expressed our belief that teaching is a fundamentally moral activity and that classrooms are places where moral values are played out. In this chapter we will argue that, to a significant extent, it is through language that the moral dimension of teaching is realized, and through language that moral meanings are negotiated in classrooms.

That language is used to express judgments, including moral judgments about beliefs and values, is obvious. Our focus here will be somewhat different: the far more subtle ways in which moral meanings are conveyed, negotiated, and interpreted through classroom discourse. It has long been acknowledged that language is central to the educational enterprise (Cazden, 1988; Halliday, 1978; Mehan, 1979), and that language, far from being a neutral device for the transfer of information, is a profoundly value-laden and ideologically colored set of codes whereby people, including teachers and learners in classrooms, mediate both relationships among themselves, and their perceptions of and actions in the real world (Bernstein, 1975, 1990, 1996; Gee, 1992, 1996, Gumperz, 1982; Wells, 1992, 1993, 1999; Wertsch, 1985, 1991). According to this view, language itself reflects many of the qualities of morality that we outlined in the previous chapter: It is an arena in which the personal and the social encounter each other, and it is one of the primary ways in which this encounter carries significance; and language, like morality, although structured by certain underlying rules, is fundamentally contingent and sensitive to context. Thus it is, for example, that many linguists have chosen to focus on spoken discourse, that is, the linguistic patterns created by groups of speakers—for example, in classroom discourse—rather than on the linguistic competence of individual speakers. For these linguists, language, like morality in our conception, exists primarily in interactions between people. We share this belief in the fundamentally social nature of language. Furthermore, we believe that it is not by coincidence that language and morality share such qualities: It is through language more than anything else that morality is played out in social situations such as classrooms.

Our examination of the moral dimensions of classroom discourse begins in a kindergarten classroom in a public elementary school. The school is located in a middle- to upper-middle-class suburb of a medium-sized city. The majority of the children attending the school are white. The few minority children in the school are African American. In this brief dialogue among the teacher (T) and the students (C1, C2, . . .), much occurs that is moral. But it is only through close examination that we arrive at answers to the following questions: What makes this discussion a moral activity? What aspects of this discussion are of moral significance? What actions, in the form of discourse moves, does the teacher make that are of moral import? How do they influence the students' responses in the discussion?

(1)	(T)	Let's see, anybody know what a buddy is?
(2)	(C1)	I know. It's somebody who you like. And it's your friend, and all, I mean . . .
(3)	(T)	Anything else? Raise your hand. Haley.
(4)	(C2)	Uh . . . somebody who you like very much.
(5)	(T)	Uh huh.
(6)	(C2)	Like me and Jeremy are.
(7)	(T)	Right. What kinds of things do buddies do together?
(8)	(C3)	Play with each other.
(9)	(T)	Play together. What are some other things that buddies can do besides play?
(10)	(C3)	Read together.
(11)	(T)	Read together. Okay.
(12)	(C4)	Do homework together.
(13)	(T)	Do homework together. Play math games together.
(14)	(C4)	Reading buddies?
(15)	(T)	Uh huh.

The moral significance of this conversation for the teacher and students has to do with the type of knowledge students acquire through participation in the activity, the role students play in the activity, the identities students construct of themselves, and the nature of the relationship between the teacher and students. These will be considered in greater detail later in the chapter. Here, though, to illustrate our point about the moral significance of classroom discourse, we will examine a single feature of this dialogue—namely, the teacher's use of repetition.

Tannen (1989) notes how repetition accomplishes a number of important functions in dialogue. Pedagogically, repetition helps individuals to comprehend the material being discussed and to make connections among the various components of the discussion. The redundancy in spoken discourse that occurs from repetition gives listeners the opportunity to receive information more slowly, thus making it easier to process and comprehend. Repetition also provides a means of linking new information with information previously introduced in the discourse. By doing so, listeners can see how the ideas are related to one another. Further, repeated sections are "intensified," which allows listeners to take more notice of the particular similarities and differences in the examples given. Repetitions by the figure in authority, the teacher, act to sanction the knowledge as important (see chapter 3). Repetition can be used to create new meanings because, through its use, the language and meanings that are repeated by the teacher come to have a shared significance and meaning for all participants in the activity. Through repetition and other linguistic patterns (see Edwards & Mercer, 1987; Tharp & Gallimore, 1988), the teacher marks certain information as shared and common knowledge (Edwards & Mercer, 1987) and certain forms of inquiry as shared forms of practice in a particular classroom.

What is the moral significance of repetition? The use of repetition is morally significant because through its use this teacher expresses her concern that the students understand both the definition of "buddy" and the way this form of inquiry works. She is conveying to the students her care and concern for the process and content of this activity and for them as individuals engaged in this activity with her. Further, we can see how the teacher guides the children in an inquiry process while gradually shifting some of the responsibility of the activity to the children. This second point bears repetition itself. Having structured the activity for the children using questions at (7) and (9), the teacher shifts the responsibility for part of the activity to the children. In a Vygotskian sense, she hands over more responsibility for and control of the activity to the children.

Finally, and perhaps most important from a moral perspective, Tannen says that repetition shows listeners that we are listening to them and hear what they are saying. Because we repeat parts of what they say, we engage in a type of *participatory listening*. Such participatory listening conveys to the students in this class not only that the teacher is listening, but that she cares about them, values their contributions, and is concerned about the way she is creating and maintaining social relationships with them.

The analysis of this dialogue brings to light two important points about the moral significance of the roles that language plays in classroom discourse. The first point is that teachers make choices about the way they conduct classroom discussions, and these choices are realized through the use of particular discourse moves. That teachers, or any speakers, make choices is of particular importance to our discussion of the moral dimensions of classroom discourse. The choices we make are of moral significance because they reflect our values and beliefs, and in doing so they reflect judgments we have made about what is important and worthwhile for our students. In short, they reflect and convey moral beliefs about teaching. Further, the choices teachers make about what to say and do in classrooms ultimately influence the quality and extent of children's participation in the activity. In other words, certain forms and patterns of classroom discourse promote certain types of learning, and thus engage children as active learners.

Other forms of classroom discourse continue to relegate students to roles as passive learners (Buzzelli, 1996). Thus, the form classroom discourse takes has important pedagogical and moral implications for the type of knowledge children acquire.

The second point is that relationships between teachers and children and among children are created and maintained through classroom discourse and, further, that the quality of the relationships is directly influenced by the form and pattern that classroom discourse takes. In sum, the ways classroom discourse is structured through the particular choices of discourse moves directly influence the nature of teaching and learning activities—that is, what the participants are doing—and also serves to structure and regulate relationships among participants. Taken together, the moral dimensions of this lesson convey important moral messages to the students. One message to students is about who they are, what they can learn, and what they should learn. Another set of moral messages has to do with how students are treated by the teacher in the activity—that is, the quality of the relationship that is created and maintained through engagement in learning activities. Clearly, classroom dialogues have important moral dimensions that warrant close study. But how are they best studied? What methods of analyzing language best uncover the often hidden moral dimensions of classroom discourse?

LANGUAGE AS MEANING MAKING— MORAL AND OTHERWISE

Language use in teaching and learning has become one of the most widely researched aspects of classroom life (see Cazden, 2001, for a review), and a variety of methods and approaches have been used to examine it. These include discourse analysis (van Dijk, 1985, 1997), critical discourse analysis (Fairclough, 1989; Luke, 1988), conversation analysis (Atkinson & Heritage, 1984), microethnography (Spindler, 1982), symbolic interactionism (Denzin, 1992), cognitive linguistics (Lakoff, 1987; Lakoff & Johnson, 1980), and sociolinguistics (Gumperz & Hymes, 1982). Each has its own strengths and weaknesses. Our examination of the moral dimensions of classroom discourse is based on the work of Michael Halliday (1978, 1993; Wells, 1993). Halliday's view of language is an ideal choice for our purposes because, according to Halliday, learning is a semiotic process—a process of making meaning—in which language plays a central role (Halliday, 1978, 1993). This view concerns itself with understanding how language is used by people, that is, "what language can do, . . . what the speaker, child or adult, can do with it" (Halliday, 1978, p. 16), rather than with developing psychological and structural explanations of language. One focus of Halliday's work has been to describe how the selection of different features of language that speakers use to express themselves—that is, the selection of particular words, phrases, and sentence forms—influences the meanings and relationships that are created by participants in an activity. In our case, those participants are teachers and students in classrooms. We believe, then, that students' engagement with different forms of classroom discourse has a differential effect on what they learn and on the relationships they create with others and, in essence, their experiences in school.

Language as a Social Semiotic

Four claims underlie Halliday's view of language as a social semiotic. The first claim is that language use is functional. The second is that the primary function of language is to create meanings. A third claims states that the social and cultural context in which the language activity occurs influences the meanings that are created and exchanged by participants in the activity. The final claim is that the semiotic process of making meaning is realized through speakers' selection of particular language features when interacting with others (Eggins, 1994).

According to Halliday, language serves three functions in our lives. The *ideational* function has to do with how we create, reflect upon, and share meanings with others. The meanings constructed through participation in activities with others are constituted, to a large extent, by the particular lexicogrammatical choices made by the participants in the activity as well as the social and cultural features of the context of the activities. The *interpersonal* function entails creating and expressing relationships among participants in an activity. Through this function language serves as a means of depicting "relations among participants in the situation, and the speaker's own intrusion into it" (Halliday, 1978, p. 46). For speakers, this function of language conveys at once the role they have chosen to assume in a particular activity and the role or roles they have designated for their listeners. Language is the means used for creating, maintaining, and changing relationships among individuals involved in dialogues. Language, literally and metaphorically, is used to move individuals into and out of roles (Davies & Hunt, 1994; O'Connor & Michaels, 1993, 1996). Lastly, the *textual* function focuses on how language is used for a particular purpose in a particular situation. Specifically, it addresses the question of whether the language used is written or oral and whether the language is constitutive of the activity or ancillary to the activity (Halliday, 1978; Halliday & Hasan, 1989).

Each of these functions contributes to what students come to know, how they are treated by teachers, and the identity they form of themselves as learners and as individuals. Because the language used in teaching can and does directly affect students as learners and individuals, it is of moral significance for teachers and students alike.

Here we want to note again that examining the moral dimensions of classroom life means we must look closely into the activities in which teachers and students engage, thereby enabling us to relate particular social and cultural features of the context of the activities to the meanings, moral and otherwise, that students create from their participation in the activities. It is important, then, for our understanding and delineation of the moral dimensions of classroom discourse that we have a means of relating the functions language serves in teaching and learning to the features of the classrooms and learning activities in which they use language. In doing so, we will be able to illuminate how the moral is present in classroom discourse.

The Context of Making Meaning

Halliday (1978) has noted that any account of language use must have built into it ways of relating variations in language use to particular features of the context in which it is used. This is particularly pertinent to our discussion of language use in teaching and learning activities because, according to Halliday and Hasan, "[l]earning is above all, a social process . . . knowledge is transmitted in social contexts . . . and the words that are exchanged in these contexts get their meaning from activities in which they are embedded" (1989, p. 5). The contexts in which language is used differ from one another in three ways: according to what is happening in the context (that is, what the participants are doing); according to who is taking part, who the participants are, and their relationship to one another; and in the role language plays in the activity. These have been referred to, respectively, as the field of discourse, the tenor of discourse, and the mode of discourse.

To relate particular dimensions of a context—namely, the field, tenor, and mode of discourse—to particular functions of language—the ideational, the interpersonal, and the textual—Halliday uses the concept of register. Register, thus, provides a means of understanding how variations in language use are related to contextual features. Halliday notes that "the register is what a person is speaking, determined by what he is doing" (1978, p. 110). Essentially, register helps us understand how our language use varies dependent upon what we are doing, who we are doing it with, our role in the activity, and the role of language in the activity. According to Wells, register is vital to our understanding of how language works in any context, because a register "looks in two directions: to the situation, and to the language as a resource for acting in the situation" (1993, p. 7). Wells goes on to note that register assists us in understanding teaching and learning as

> the collaborative behavior of two or more participants as they use the meaning potential of a shared language to mediate the establishment and achievement of their goals in social action. In order to be successful in this endeavor, they must negotiate a common interpretation of the situation in terms of field, tenor, and mode, and . . . they must make appropriate choices from their linguistic resources in terms of the ideational, interpersonal and textual metafunctions. (1993, p. 8)

Of central importance to us is that the moral dimensions of classroom discourse come into sharper focus when we examine the register of the language of teaching and learning. When we look at the field of discourse of teaching and learning activities, which reveals the nature of the activities in which the participants are engaged and how language is used as a resource for them, we can ask the following questions: How is language being used to structure and carry out the activity? What are the teacher's goals in the activity? What types of knowledge are being acquired from the activity? How does involvement in this activity contribute to the types of persons and learners they become?

Similarly, an examination of the tenor of discourse will reveal how language functions to position speakers in relation to each other and to assign a role to each participant. The positioning and the assignment of individuals to different roles involves the relative distribution of power and status among participants. Differences in the relative distribution of power and status in turn contribute to the development of different types of knowledge and different identities by students. Our examination of tenor addresses the following questions: How is language used to create relationships between the teacher and students in a particular classroom? How is language used to create, define, and maintain the roles and status of teachers and students in activities? How does language serve to relegate some students to certain types of roles and status? By examining the tenor of discourse and the interpersonal function of language, we gain insights into the moral nature of the relationships created and maintained in classrooms. For it is within the relationships that we can see how the roles to which students are assigned and the status each is afforded contribute to the quality of their experience in the classroom.

One purpose of presenting this discussion was to describe the functions language serves in teaching and learning. A second purpose was to examine how the construct of register provides us with a deep view into the functions of language by relating those functions to particular aspects of the context in which the language is being used. Finally, we wanted to set forth our claim that a closer examination of the functions of language using register can bring to the foreground the moral significance of classroom discourse. The questions posed are as much about moral issues as they are about pedagogical issues. We turn now to providing some answers to these questions by examining transcripts of several classroom dialogues.

REGISTER ANALYSIS: A CLOSER LOOK AT THE MORAL DIMENSIONS OF CLASSROOM DISCOURSE

As Halliday has noted, "language comes to life only when functioning in some environment. We do not experience language in isolation—if we did we would not recognize it as language—but always in relation to a scenario, some background of persons and actions and events from which the things which are said derive their meaning" (1978, p. 28). With this in mind, let us revisit the kindergarten classroom introduced at the beginning of the chapter, where the teacher (T) and children (C1, C2, . . .) are discussing what a buddy is. Our objective here is to use the construct of register to analyze this excerpt of classroom dialogue. We will emphasize how such an analysis can highlight the moral dimensions of this dialogue.

(1)	(T)	Let's see, anybody know what a buddy is?
(2)	(C1)	I know. It's somebody who you like. And it's your friend, and all, I mean . . .
(3)	(T)	Anything else? Raise your hand. Haley.
(4)	(C2)	Uh . . . somebody who you like very much.
(5)	(T)	Uh huh.
(6)	(C2)	Like me and Jeremy are.
(7)	(T)	Right. What kinds of things do buddies do together?
(8)	(C3)	Play with each other.
(9)	(T)	Play together. What are some other things that buddies can do besides play?
(10)	(C3)	Read together.
(11)	(T)	Read together. Okay.
(12)	(C4)	Do homework together.
(13)	(T)	Do homework together. Play math games together.
(14)	(C4)	Reading buddies?
(15)	(T)	Uh huh.

At the beginning of this chapter we briefly examined the moral dimensions of this dialogue as an example of how classroom discourse is of moral significance to teachers and students. Here we will present a more detailed analysis of the discourse, to get a better sense of what is happening in the activity. Then we will show how an examination of the field and tenor of this dialogue can bring its moral dimension into sharper focus.

The dialogue begins with the teacher addressing the entire class with the question: "Anybody know what a buddy is?" followed by an initial response at (2) "It's somebody who you like." The teacher's question at (3) "Anything else?" simultaneously acknowledges the student's response at (2) as acceptable in content and form while requesting more responses. Because this response is acknowledged and accepted by the teacher, other children at (4), (8), (10), and (12) proceed to add to the list that defines a buddy. As the discussion continues, the teacher affirms each response at (7), (9) and (11), and tags on a question whose purpose is to extend or clarify the child's response. So, for example, after C2 notes that buddies are "Like me and Jeremy," the teacher at (7) affirms this and then moves the discussion further along, asking, "What kinds of things do buddies do together?" Following C3's response at (8), "Play with each other," the teacher again affirms and asks for an expansion of the comment at (9): "What are some other things that buddies can do besides play?" By requesting that students expand and clarify their responses, the teacher seeks to add depth and complexity to the definition of buddy, and in this way illustrates to students that a good definition *has* depth and complexity. At (11) and (13) the teacher only repeats the child's response, leaving off the question. By omitting the question that previously served to guide the children's responses, the teacher assumes that the students have an implicit understanding of how the process of constructing the definition works. It appears that the students have an understanding of this process, as at (12) and (14) they continue to offer examples of what buddies do together. The dialogue ends at (15) with the teacher's acknowledgment of C4's response at (14).

Young (1992), using Halliday's (1978) notion of register, presents a schematic way of examining how the different values of the field of discourse are related to the different forms of knowledge that students acquire as a result of participation in the learning activities, and how the different values of tenor

Child:	Practicing, listening, reproducing	Doing, stating, theorizing
	I————————————————————————I	
Teacher:	Telling, testing, task setting	Raising questions, facilitating

Figure 1

are related to the variations in the nature of the relationships that are created between teacher and students.

On the continuum in figure 1 (adapted from Young, 1992, p. 89), different values of field are shown corresponding to different activities undertaken by the teacher and students. The activities engaged in by the teacher (T) below the dotted line are paralleled by those of the students (S) shown above the dotted line. The different activities reflect a variety of types of involvement by the students, from active inquirers to passive respondents, and the related types of learning and knowledge gained from the various forms of engagement. The buddy dialogue exemplifies the right side of the continuum. Questions and responses by the teacher seek to expand students' comments, ask for clarification, or encourage further discussion (Buzzelli, 1996; Wells, 1993). As the example illustrates and as depicted in figure 1, the teacher is raising questions and facilitating the discussion. As a result students are active participants in stating their views and in the "doing" of defining a buddy.

Field

We can observe from the dialogue how the activity of defining a buddy has been jointly constructed as the continual process of adding to the list of activities that buddies do together. With the teacher's guidance, the students construct a definition of a buddy. It is accomplished in such a way that the definition is part of the shared or common knowledge of the class members (Edwards & Mercer, 1987). We can see this in how the follow-up questions at (7) and (9) serve to outline a method of inquiry and a process for defining words. At the same time, the students are apprenticed into a form of inquiry, a way of thinking about and seeking information. Had the children been told the definition, they would indeed know "what a buddy is," but they would not have been actively involved in the inquiry process; rather, they would have been involved in listening and reproducing, as indicated on the left side of the continuum. The analysis of this dialogue illustrates how a particular form of discourse is used to create a particular type of teaching and learning activity. For this teacher and these students, this form of discourse has taken on a specific meaning for constructing a definition of a buddy and for how one conducts inquiry. That students engage in this activity as active learners sends a powerful moral message to them about their teacher's expectations of them as students and learners. More is expected and more is attained from these students than in classrooms where teachers tell students what they need to know, leaving students to play a more passive role in their education. It is a moral message about their identities as students and learners, that the teacher has high expectations of them for both the present lesson and their participation in future lessons.

An analysis of a second dialogue, which represents the left side of the continuum, will illustrate how language can function quite differently. The differences between these two examples will highlight how different forms of dialogue create different teaching and learning experiences and different moral meanings. The second example, a discussion about sinking and floating that takes place among teacher (T) and six four- and five-year-old children (P1, P2, ...), is taken from Hughes and Westgate (1988, p. 11).

(1) (T) Now we're going to find out things that will . . . ?

(2) (Chorus) Float.

(3)	(T)	Float. And things that will . . . ?
(4)	(Chorus)	Sink.
(5)	(T)	Sink. How many of these will float?
(6)	(P1)	A boat will.
(7)	(T)	How does a boat float?
(8)	(P2)	It just floats there.
(9)	(T)	How do you know it is floating? (Pause) Does it go under the water or does it stay on top of the water?
(10)	(P2)	On top.
(11)	(T)	It stays on top of the water.

On the surface it appears that students are actively engaged in the discourse and that learning is taking place in the lesson. The teacher's questions, it might seem, serve as a scaffold for the students' learning by providing prompts that assist them in creating their own understandings of the activity at hand (Vygotsky, 1978; Wood, Bruner, & Ross, 1976). In actuality, the heavy use of clues leads the students to the answers, but they are ritual answers (Edwards & Mercer, 1987) that belie any conceptual understanding of the process being studied.

One aspect of this exchange that immediately stands out is the short length of the answers at (2), (4), and (10). Indeed, with the exception of (8), none is more than a phrase. A number of reasons may account for this. The questions at (1) and (3) are phrased as leading questions in that they are constructed for a specific, one-and-only response. The questions have two other features. First, in asking these questions, the teacher seems to be assuming that the students already know the answers. Such questions are often referred to as "known answer questions" (Mehan, 1979; Young, 1992). Although ostensibly functioning as a tool for teaching, actually such questions more often serve to assess students' knowledge and present level of understanding. They are display questions through which students demonstrate their existing knowledge.

The second feature is the fill-in-blanks quality of the questions evident at (1), (3), and (9). This is especially characteristic of the initiation-response-evaluation (IRE) format (Mehan, 1979) common to many classrooms. The IRE pattern—which also has been labeled initiation-response-feedback (IRF; Stubbs & Robinson, 1979), triadic dialogue (Lemke, 1985, 1990), and "Guess What the Teacher Knows" (GWTK; Young, 1992)—consists of an initial question from the teacher, followed by a student's response (answer) to the question, which in turn is followed by the teacher's evaluation or follow-up to the student's response. The result of this pattern is that children are confined to contributing exactly what the teacher requests, with little or no opportunity to express or expand upon their own ideas. In this short sequence, then, the teacher appears to maintain a rather tight control over the dialogue and, in turn, over the students' responses through use of known-answer questions.

The teacher's goal in this example is one of telling students what they need to know and then assessing their ability to reproduce it. This type of dialogue results from an evaluative move in the "third turn" (Buzzelli, 1996; Wells, 1993). The field of the activity entails task setting, telling, and testing on the part of the teacher, whereas the students are involved in reproducing, listening, and practicing what they know. Because the teacher already knows the answers to the questions, the purpose of the discourse is to gauge the students' level of understanding of the concepts of sink and float.

A comparison of the two examples shows that a number of different features are present in the first dialogue, features that mark it as a richer experience for teacher and students alike and that are absent in the second dialogue. In the buddy example, students are actively engaged in constructing the definition. On the other hand, in the sink/float example, students are responding to well-defined questions that seek specific answers. Here, too, the students are apprenticed into a form of inquiry, but one that relies on reception of information from others. Further, we can see from these two dialogues how different forms of discourse are related to different values of the field and to the different forms of knowledge that students acquire as a result of participation in the learning activities. Edwards and Mercer (1987) refer to the knowledge represented on the right side of the continuum as principled knowledge, knowledge that is "essentially explanatory, oriented towards an understanding of how procedures and processes work, of why certain conclusions are necessary or valid" (Edwards & Mercer, 1987, p. 97). Knowledge acquired from activities represented on the left side of the continuum is referred to as ritual knowledge—that is, merely knowing what to say or what to do when asked by the teacher.

The continuum of field offers a means of examining how language is used to "get things done" in the lesson (Halliday, 1978; Wells, 1993). It illustrates how different forms of dialogue shape different types of experiences for the students, experiences in which they acquire different forms of knowledge and are apprenticed into different forms of inquiry. More significantly, however, it illustrates quite graphically that the differences are qualitative and, as such, are moral in nature. Clearly, the children in each activity are learning different forms of knowledge and different forms of inquiry. That some students are able to engage in the activity as active learners, whereas others are passive recipients, sends a powerful moral message to the students about their teacher's expectations of them as students and learners, but also about the type of persons they could become. To put it another way, the moral message to students is about who they are, what they can learn, and what they can be. Clearly, when examining the two dialogues, we see how students in one classroom are treated differently from those in the other classroom. In one classroom more is expected and more is attained than in the other. Our examination of discourse, though, is not only about what is expected and what is learned. Another aspect of the moral import of the activity is how students are treated by the teacher in the activity—that is, the quality of the relationship that is created and maintained through engagement in learning activities—and this has to do with the tenor of discourse.

Tenor

Young (1992) also considers how variations in forms of discourse are related to different values of tenor. Tenor is that aspect of register which addresses the participants in the activity, the roles they assume or are assigned in the activity, and the relationship they have to each other. Different forms of discourse contribute to the creation and enactment of different types of relationships among the teacher and students in a classroom. The nature of the relationships affords the teacher and students different roles and status in the classroom, thereby influencing the quality and degree of engagement of both in teaching and learning activities. Ultimately, both the nature of the relationships between a teacher and students and the level of engagement in learning activities attained by students can greatly influence the images students create of themselves as learners. These are illustrated in figure 2 (adapted from Young, 1992).

The teacher's role in the buddy discourse, as represented in the tenor of discourse, is that of facilitator and guide. Her repetitions keep the dialogue going while serving to clarify, expand, and evaluate the children's responses. Although she does not tell them outright what a buddy is, she guides their construction of the definition. The role ascribed to the students is that of active co-constructor of the definition. The students provide exemplars of a buddy, to which the teacher responds. Finally, we consider the social distance between the teacher and students as another marker of tenor. Although the

Child:	Child as learning object	Child as subject of learning
	I———————————————————I	
Teacher:	Teacher as teller	Teacher as guide

Figure 2

roles of teacher and student are well defined, the teacher's comments and questions are clearly responsive to the comments of the students. In other words, the teacher takes her cues from the students' comments and suggestions, which makes for an easy give-and-take among all participants. The contributions of all are valued in the construction of the definition. This style of dialogue indicates a relatively low amount of social distance between teacher and students.

The sink/float discourse provides a rather different view. The teacher engages the children in a series of short-answer questions. The questions serve to establish her role and position as the provider of information and as the evaluator of knowledge. The relationship between teacher and students created by this form of dialogue is hierarchical, with the role of each clearly and rigidly defined; the teacher asks questions and the students provide answers. This creates a relatively large social distance between teacher and students. As a result, the roles of the teacher and students and the hierarchical nature of the roles are reified.

This examination of the tenor of these two dialogues provides insights into the nature of the relationships that are created and enacted between the teachers and students in these two classrooms. The differences are reflected in who and what each teacher cares about and how that care is expressed to the students in her room. Other things being equal, we would want to see children of our own in the classroom featuring the buddy discourse. However, our purpose in this analysis is not to suggest that one teacher is more caring of her students than the other, nor that one teacher is more moral than the other. Rather, we wish to show that the differences in the two forms of caring, how the teacher cares, and what the teacher cares about convey different moral messages to the students about who they are as students, learners, and persons in each room.

Our examination of the moral dimensions of these dialogues using field and tenor gives us an appreciation of how teaching practices as embodied in forms of classroom discourse and curricula function not only to instruct students but also to regulate students' thinking and behavior; that is, they regulate what students learn, how they learn, and the types of students and learners they are and will become. In this sense, they add to our understanding of the regulatory process of classroom discourse whereby "the transmitter learns to be a transmitter and the acquirer learns to be an acquirer" (Bernstein, 1990, p. 65). With this in mind we can ask two important questions: How can we examine the moral dimensions of the instructional and regulatory functions of classroom discourse? And what are the moral implications for teachers and students of the patterns of interaction and organizational practices (Daniels, 1989) embedded in the teaching methods and curricula enacted in classrooms through dialogue? The influence of classroom discourse on children's thinking and activity has been the subject of Basil Bernstein's research, especially his notion of pedagogical discourse, for the past 30 years. It is to his work that we turn now.

PEDAGOGIC DISCOURSE: EMBEDDING INSTRUCTIONAL DISCOURSE IN THE MORAL DISCOURSE

Over the years in a number of his writings Bernstein (1975, 1990, 1996) has outlined the notion of pedagogic discourse. What Bernstein refers to as pedagogic discourse is the principle whereby the competencies and knowledge to be acquired (that is, what the students are to learn) are embedded in the forms of language and teaching practices used by the teacher to regulate the students' behavior in the classroom. Bernstein refers to the former as the *instructional discourse* and the latter, which "legitimizes the official rules regulating order, relation and identity" (1990, p. 188), as the *regulative discourse*. Pedagogic discourse, then, leads to "the embedding of one discourse in another, to create one text, to create *one* discourse"

(1996, p. 46). He notes that the two are often separated as the instructional and the moral:

> Often people in schools and in classrooms make a distinction between what they call the transmission of skills and the transmission of values. . . . Most researchers are continually studying the two, or thinking as if there are two: as if education is about values on the one hand, and about competence on the other. In my view there are not two discourses, there is only one. . . . The regulative discourse is the dominant discourse . . . this is obvious because it is the *moral* discourse that creates the criteria which give rise to character, manner, conduct. . . . In school it tells children what to do, where they can go. (1996, pp. 46–48).

Bernstein views the regulative discourse as the moral discourse because it creates "a moral regulation of the social relations of transmission/acquisition, that is, rules of order, relation and identity, and . . . such a moral order is prior to, and a condition for, the transmission of competencies" (1990, p. 184). Bernstein summarizes these relationships, noting that "[p]edagogic discourse . . . embeds competence in order and order in competence or, more generally, consciousness in conscience and conscience in consciousness" (1990, p. 185). It is important to note here that the regulation Bernstein talks about is the type of regulation that occurs in all classrooms. This is an essential point of Bernstein's concept of pedagogic discourse. The regulation of students' thinking and behavior is an inherent feature of the discourse of instruction. Indeed, instruction does not occur without such regulation, and it is through Bernstein's insightful work that this is brought to our attention. This is also one of the central points of this chapter: coming to an understanding and appreciation of how such regulation is embedded in classroom discourse.

An examination of another sample of classroom dialogue will illustrate and clarify the points we outlined above. The dialogue was recorded in a third-grade classroom during an author's chair activity. During this activity, the students take turns reading stories they had written. After the reading of each story, the author asks fellow students if they have comments or questions about the story. In the incident below, Robbie is just about to begin reading his story.

(1) T: All right, Robbie. Go ahead.
(2) Robbie: Okay. I'm gonna start a new ch—story, because my other one, I had so many misspelled words, and, um, I ha—, in my first chapter is at jammin' gym, and I just started on it today, and, here I go! (Begins reading.) Joey, come on. If we are going to jammin' gym, we have got to go now. I have rented a limo to take us there. Okay. Let's go. The limo is here. We are on our way. Joey said, "Hey guy, up in the front, where's the beer?" Under the seat. Joey, move out of the way. AAAAHH! Joe's hanging out the window. And that's all I said. (*Class claps.*) Response. (*Children put their hands up.*) Jessica.
(3) Jessica: How in the world did Joey get out, hanging out the window?
(4) Robbie: Because I pushed, I knocked him out of the way and he hit the door, and he's hanging off the door, outside, and we're going a hundred miles per hour on the freeway. He's hanging by his pinkies, and then we go up to a hundred and ten and he falls out the window. Chris?
(5) Chris: Um, well, this is just a suggestion, all right, um, oh, I'm just supposed to ask one question. . . . Are y'all gonna get caught drinking that beer?

(6)   Robbie: He is. Well, actually, he's going to get arrested because he falls out the window and he rolls a couple of feet and then goes up to the bank and he goes where all the money's hid, and then he breaks in, and then he goes to jail. And then that's when the real funny part's going to be. When we go to jail. When HE goes to jail. (*To group asking to see who is to share next or for a final question*): Anybody? (*Students point and mumble among themselves.*) Kate.

(7)   Kate: No. . . .

(8)   T: Uh, before Robbie leaves I want to discuss some little something that—I'm wondering if, what you thought about. Just—when he used the word *beer* in the story, uh, I'm wondering, how do y'all feel about that?

(9)   Mark: Some kinds of beer are good for you.

(10)   Robbie: It's alcohol. It's nonalcohol.

(11)   Mark: You know, like root beer, it's not alcohol.

(12)   T: Well, that wasn't said.

(13)   Mark: He can . . .

(14)   T: That wasn't said, see.

(15)   Robbie: I can change it to that.

(16)   T: Well, I'm just thinking, you know like, uh. What would be acceptable as far as words that we use here at school? And, uh, what are your thoughts on it? (*Whispering among children: "It's okay," "I don't like it," "I don't think"; Will, standing near the teacher, says something.*)

(17)   T: Wait a minute, turn around and tell everybody.

(18)   Will: I don't like the wor–when he uses beer in the story. It's sort of a slang word, especially if it's a kid's story that you'll be reading to

		a class. I mean, grown-ups, like, if you were reading a grown-up book, you'd probably find some stuff like that in it, but not in a kid's story.
(19)	Mark:	I know, if he changed it to root beer, it'd be SAFE.
(20)	Chris:	Safe?
(21)	Ann:	I used to drink root beer.
		(*Robbie makes an inaudible comment.*)
(22)	Clare:	Well, what if it gets public? I mean, it'll give children the idea to do it.
(23)	Marie:	I know, and it'll influence them.
		(*Most students look toward the teacher.*)
(24)	T:	Okay. Well, I don't ever really want to make a person change their words or their thoughts in a story, but just every once in a while something kind of comes up, maybe a word that maybe is, might offend somebody else in the room or might, like Emily said—Emily, what was it you just said about . . . ?
(25)	Clare:	It might get published one day, and if you like . . . children . . . encourage them to do it.
(26)	T:	In other words, it might influence somebody. And again, I don't ever want to make you change something, but I just wanted to hear your thoughts on it because there's certain subjects that, uh, might or might not be acceptable to children.

In this brief exchange the teacher is faced with a dilemma that is both complex and moral in nature. It involves a struggle between enacting her beliefs about teaching—that is, how to nurture children's emerging voices and skills as authors—while at the same time considering the implications of her actions—

namely, the influence that children's words and stories may have on others. The struggle is heightened for both teacher and students because it occurs during an author's chair activity, during which children share stories they have written. It is a discourse that involves regulating behavior, order, and children's identities as writers. Our intent is to examine how the content of writing instruction is embedded within a discussion of conduct and social order. It involves the ways the teacher seeks to guide, to instruct, and, in effect, to regulate students' behavior.

The teacher first raises the issue of the word *beer* at (8). Robbie, noting the concern, attempts to change the meaning, saying at (10) "It's nonalcohol." However, the teacher refers back to the text twice for clarification; at (12), "Well, that wasn't said," and at (14), "That wasn't said, see." At this point in the dialogue, we see how the regulatory discourse turns upon itself as the teacher's reference to the original text of the story serves to regulate aspects of the discussion. This is followed at (15) with Robbie's saying, "I can change it to that." The teacher does not directly address this suggestion, perhaps leaving Robbie wondering why it is rejected. At (16) the teacher wonders aloud, "What would be acceptable . . . here at school?" and then asks for the students' thoughts. This section of the dialogue is interesting for several reasons. In wondering aloud about what is acceptable, a message is sent to students that there are aspects of writing which must be regulated, and that the regulation must be done by them as authors. This goes beyond the mechanics of writing; it is about considering the moral consequences of their work. Second, although the teacher wants them to express their ideas through writing and story telling, she is calling their attention to the norms that define what is acceptable at school. In asking for their thoughts, the teacher continues to reinforce the notion that the regulation of content should be guided by norms of what is acceptable in school, the students' understanding of those norms, and (although not specifically mentioned but certainly related to the preceding point), the student's own conscience.

At this point in the discussion the teacher is saying to the students that an important part of being a good writer involves being a responsible writer, and that this responsibility entails maintaining an awareness of what is appropriate for a particular context—in this case, the classroom. In making this point, the teacher embeds learning how to write in the broader framework of using one's conscience to regulate and guide what one writes. In essence, then, the teacher's statement is part of a regulatory discourse, which has embedded within it the instructional discourse concerning learning how to write. The discussion that follows serves as evidence that the students are understanding the process. Indeed, this discussion causes Mark at (19) to make the point that "if he changed it to root beer, it'd be safe." This point is considered for a few turns. Clare's comment at (22), in which she wonders what would happen "if it gets public? I mean, it'll give children the idea to do it," and Marie's comment at (23) that "it'll influence them," seem to indicate that the teacher's comment at (16) has stirred students to reflect upon the influence their writings can have on others. In effect, the teacher has made the students conscious of the role of their conscience in writing.

Up to this point our discussion has focused on the dialogue as a moral activity—namely, that it is a discourse about regulating behavior, order, and children's identities as writers. As we continue our analysis, we hear how the teacher makes her personal struggle public when she comments at (24), "Well, I don't ever really want to make a person change their words or their thoughts in a story, but just every once in a while something kind of comes up, maybe a word that maybe is, might offend somebody else in the room," and at (26), "And again, I don't ever want to make you change something, but I just wanted to hear your thoughts on it because there's certain subjects that, uh, might or might not be acceptable to children." From these two comments, it is evident that the teacher wants the students to find and express their own voices but not to offend others. On the other hand, she is acutely aware of and sensitive to avoiding asking them to change their words, thoughts, and voice. Such sensitivity is evident in her reluctance to let Robbie change his words, in spite of his offer to do so. It is as though she senses that Robbie's offer may have resulted from her raising the topic of his using the word *beer*. This appears to be how she resolves the struggle.

Through our analysis of this dialogue, we have considered how the students are being instructed in two important aspects of writing, and how to strike a balance between the two. One aspect has to do with the expression of one's voice as an author; the second aspect involves both an awareness and an acknowledgment of the effects of one's writing on the audience. The children are asked to be conscious of the effects of their writing upon others, thereby embedding an awareness of their own writing process in the consideration of the effect of the story's contents on others. Thus, the instructional discourse, with its function of developing competencies—in this case, nurturing children's emerging skills as writers and the expression of their voices—is embedded in the regulative discourse that functions to maintain social order, manner, and conduct by telling children to write so as not to offend or influence others in negative ways. Here we see, in Bernstein's words, the embedding of consciousness in conscience and conscience in consciousness.

Bernstein's notion of pedagogic discourse also provides a framework through which we can see how field and tenor become ways of understanding what he calls the social grammar of discourse. Thus, in our earlier examination of field and tenor, we saw their role in creating activities and relationships. Now we can consider how field and tenor also act in a regulatory role in discourse.

As we consider the field of this discourse, it is evident that over the course of the discussion there is a shift in the goal of the activity. What starts out as an author's chair activity, in which students share their writing with other students, quickly becomes a discussion of learning how writers struggle with important aspects of the writing process. The teacher expresses her concern that the children learn to be competent, conscious, and conscientious writers. The central focus of the activity is on learning how to balance expressing one's voice (that is, telling one's story) while at the same time being aware of and sensitive to the influence one's words may have on others. Parallel to this activity is the teacher's own struggle with just this issue. For her, the activity has become one of balancing her respect for the author's words as written and her concern for how those words can affect others. Thus, the activity is ultimately concerned with the moral implications of the teacher's struggle with regulating her own actions as a teacher and how those actions involve her possible regulation of students' writing in her class.

How is this regulation expressed through the tenor of the discourse? We hear in the discussion how the teacher expresses great care for the relationship she shares with the students and that they all share with the texts the students have written. The teacher has created and seeks to maintain relationships with the students that allow her to exercise her role as the authority in the classroom and as an authority on writing. The teacher's role, then, is at once as instructor and as regulator. The teacher models the behavior of each role for the students and in doing so helps create with the students their own roles as writers. Within each role, however, the teacher assumes responsibility for the students. On the one hand, the students will not be offended or negatively influenced by others' words. On the other hand, their texts will not be summarily changed. The roles are hierarchical and complementary.

In this analysis we have examined how the teacher's questioning and commenting during the beer dialogue conveys messages to students about their responsibilities as authors. Indeed, the central moral message seems to be that as authors they have a dual responsibility: a responsibility to themselves as authors to express their own ideas and voice and a responsibility to their readers to be conscious of the effects of their writing on the audience. In this dialogue, then, we see and hear how the discourse of competencies of writing is embedded within the discourse on the responsibilities of writing—that is, the discourse on social order and conduct.

Our analysis of the field and tenor could be undertaken in much more depth and detail. Our intent here is to illustrate the multilayered nature of classroom discourse. Each layer offers a different perspective on how language is used in teaching and learning. Each layer also adds to the moral complexity of teaching and learning.

CONCLUSION: HEARING THE MORAL IN CLASSROOM DISCOURSE

In this chapter we have looked at how language is used in classrooms. We have considered dialogues as particular moral events, and our discussion of them has focused on the specific moral meanings these particular dialogues may have for teachers and children. But the meanings of specific dialogues must not draw our attention away from the realization that dialogues—repeated again and again, throughout the day, and day after day—become representative of broader, general pedagogical practices and curricula whose moral meaning for teachers and children must also be considered. Young's (1984, 1988, 1990, 1992) critique of the ways discourse is used in classrooms foregrounds for us the moral aspects of teaching and learning by focusing our attention on the meaning of these experiences for students' learning and development (Buzzelli, 1996).

Throughout this chapter we have seen how different forms of dialogue influence the extent of students' participation in learning activities and the particular roles afforded to them as participants. Both greatly affect the types of knowledge they gain through participation in learning activities and the identities they create for themselves as learners and as individuals

(Buzzelli, 1996). Examining classroom discourse, then, can provide us with a framework for a broader analysis of teaching practices and curricula. It is our hope that the framework outlined in this chapter can provide teachers and teacher educators with a means of addressing the moral complexity and moral ambiguity they encounter in their classrooms. Broadly conceived, the moral complexity and moral ambiguity teachers encounter are about how to teach in pedagogically *and* morally sound ways.

In this chapter we have addressed only a few of the many moral issues raised by an examination of language in the classroom. These issues are of crucial importance for teachers and teacher educators. One of our goals was to provide a framework for viewing classroom discourse through a moral lens. In so doing, we wanted to move questions about what is moral in classrooms to the foreground. It is our hope that the framework can provide a means of reading and hearing the many moral signs that lie below the surface in classroom discourse, but whose significance is enormous in the lives of teachers and students.

We end at the place were we began, by noting that classroom discourse is fundamentally a moral arena for teachers and students. Language is inherently social and, as a social phenomenon, it is also inherently moral. Examining the underlying dynamics of language for the ways that it creates and regulates knowledge, relationships, and identity not only brings our attention to the central aspect of language as a moral medium in the classroom but also leads us to consider the extent to which teachers have power and authority over students through teaching practices and curricula. In the next chapter we turn our moral lens to the issues of power and authority, which, like language, seem to lie just below the surface of classroom life but have a profound influence on children's learning and development.

THREE

Morality and Power
in the Classroom

INTRODUCTION

We have established thus far that classrooms are places of moral action and interaction, and that the moral dimension of classroom life is complex and multivalued. Furthermore, in the previous chapter we argued that to a significant extent the morality of teaching is mediated through the language used by teachers and learners in their work together. In the present chapter, we want to suggest that *power* is another crucial component in moral relations between teacher and students.

Just as with language and with morality itself, the notion of power is best understood as something that resides neither entirely within an individual nor in the group, but rather in the complex interplay between them; like language, it is both personal and social. It is thus misleading to say that someone (for example, the teacher) "has" power; but it also is misleading to suggest that invisible "power structures" predetermine our relations. Rather, as with language, individual agency exists alongside constraining social forces, making relations of power a complex series of negotiations in which everyone participates. Thus, along with language, power is an important way in which relations in a group (such as a class) are mediated.

At the same time, power is a constant in classrooms, as in all other arenas of social life. As we will explain in more detail below, it is not possible to "remove" power relations from education. Through increased awareness and careful adjustment, power relations in classrooms and schools can be changed for the better; but it is a mistake to see power as an evil that needs to be combated. In this chapter we will work from the assumption that power in teaching, in one form or another, is here to stay.

The central argument of this chapter is that *power relations in teaching are fundamentally moral in nature.* Whatever your view of power in education—whether you are an authoritarian, a critical pedagogist, or (like the great majority of teachers) somewhere in between—power relations are profoundly imbued with questions of values, beliefs, and notions of what is right and wrong, good and bad—in short, with moral significance. The bulk of this chapter will be devoted to an examination of the nature of this significance in certain areas of teaching in which power relations are particularly starkly delineated.

What does it mean to say that power relations in education are moral in nature? Let's take a very straightforward example. A thumbnail definition of power is "the ability of A to get B to do something that B would otherwise not do" (Maxwell, 1991, p. 142). Getting B to do something B would not normally do is exactly what teachers do all day, every day. Of course, it will be objected that some children will do some things without prompting, and we acknowledge this to be true. But if we are honest we will admit that, however organized and driven our students are, the vast majority of activities in which children engage in classrooms would almost certainly not take place without the teacher's involvement. Even in explicitly nonteacher-centered approaches like Whole Language, the teacher still has a vital role as organizer and provider of resources and direction, without which the process of learning would be, at the very least, severely impaired. Even in these approaches, ultimately, the teacher is still getting children to do things they would not otherwise do. This can be seen much more clearly, of course, in more directive kinds of teaching.

The point is that it is precisely in these actions of the teacher that the moral significance of teaching is to be found. A (the teacher) gets B (the student) to do things that B would not otherwise do because, in A's view, *it is the right thing to do*. The assumption that, even when B does not want to do this thing, it is truly in B's best interests to do it, that B will benefit from doing it, and that (sooner or later) B will not resent this imposition but will be grateful for it, is a moral assumption. It is in this assumption that we can most clearly see the intimate connection between power and morality in teaching: The teacher's goal in changing the students involves at once moral action and the exercise of power.

Morality and power are intertwined in all aspects of power relations in classrooms, however the relationship is played out. Below, we will explore the notion of *authority* as a way of revealing how power and morality coexist in classrooms and what the teacher's role in this relationship is. For the moment, let us simply underline the fact that issues of morality and issues of power are virtually coextensive with classroom interaction.

In this chapter, we will precede our discussion with a more detailed explanation of our understanding of power. The greater part of the chapter will then look at four specific aspects of educational work in which the relationship between power and morality is vividly seen. First, we will consider the dual meaning of authority in teaching. Then, we will look at the moral meaning of assessment practices, focusing on grading and examinations. The latter topic will lead us into a consideration of the physical control of bodies (ranging from corporal punishment to seating arrangements), in which the deployment of power also has an important moral dimension. Finally, we will look at more subtle ways in which the exercise of power is morally charged, focusing on the linked issues of voice and dialogue in classroom interactions.

These are, however, merely instantiations of the broader point we want to convey. Our claim is that in *every* aspect of power relations there is a crucial moral component—indeed, the moral element is the most important thing about the way power is used and negotiated in the classroom. Furthermore, like use of language, power relations are imbued with complex and multivalent moral significance; and, like language, power relations exist first and foremost in action and in specific contexts between particular individuals and groups.

POWER IN EDUCATION

The conception of power outlined above is not radically new. For us, it has become clarified by following a particular line of research and theory in the education literature. In the present section we will briefly outline this literature. This is not a comprehensive literature review but a highly selective history intended to trace the roots of the position taken in this chapter.

To begin with, there is a venerable tradition of critique of the significant social forces that are brought to play on power relations in classrooms and schools. Writers from Young (1971) and Bernstein (1975) to Apple (1982) and beyond have depicted the school as a societal institution that serves in the ongoing reproduction of existing power relations, and hence inequities, prejudices, and so on. In the view of these scholars, the aim of schooling is to produce "good" citizens (here the moral already makes an appearance)—that is, citizens who do what they are told and serve in their turn to replicate the state as it stands. Part of this process involves the reproduction of legitimate forms of knowledge. As Apple puts it succinctly, "Schools allocate people and legitimate knowledge. They legitimate people and allocate knowledge" (Apple, 1982, p. 42).

There is simply too much evidence in support of this view to dismiss it, and we believe that Apple and his colleagues are basically right in their analysis of this aspect of power relations at a systemic level in education. Yet, although these structures clearly are major forces to be reckoned with, it is important not to lose sight of the agency of the individual teacher. This theme has been taken up by a related line of inquiry and argumentation, that of critical pedagogy. Critical pedagogists concur with the ideological analyses referred to above; yet they call for an active role for teachers in explicitly counteracting the reproductive (and hence oppressive) agenda of the school and the broader society in which the school is situated (Giroux, 1988; McLaren, 1989). Perceiving education as fundamentally political in nature (i.e., concerned above all with power), critical pedagogists suggest that, in light of this view of teaching, political action is an imperative for the teacher, and they call upon teachers to empower students and to work in "radical" ways for the goals of social justice and equity.

Yet critical pedagogy alone cannot provide a full or accurate understanding of the operation of power in classrooms and schools. First, critical pedagogy has itself been criticized by many. It has been suggested, by Ellsworth (1989), for example, that critical pedagogy has engendered its own orthodoxy and hierarchy, and that its elitist use of language and overly optimistic vision of democratic classrooms is ultimately exclusive and disempowering from the point of view of the students themselves, and of their teachers too (Janangelo, 1993). Gore (1996) suggests that radical pedagogies in general lead to the enactment of "new regimes of truth" (p. 6) that are eerily reminiscent of the accounts mentioned earlier of knowledge control in mainstream education by Apple (1982) and others.

Another objection that has been raised against critical pedagogy, and one that is directly relevant to the subject of the present chapter, is that it encourages a simplistic view of power and power relations. To talk in terms of "taking" and "giving" power implies a view of power as a commodity or object that can be passed from hand to hand. Our own view of power in classrooms is much more in line with Foucault's depiction of power as something that "circulates"—something that is not "held" by individuals but is constructed and negotiated by all (Foucault, 1980). According to Foucault, power exists first and foremost in relations between people. It is neither social structures nor individuals that determine power relations; rather, power relations are enacted and reinforced by the very people who take part in them—that is, people are "caught up in a power situation of which they themselves are the bearers" (1977, p. 201).

Foucault's account of power has been lent strong support by empirical research conducted by Gore (1994, 1996). Gore studied power relations in four different kinds of classroom, including traditional and "radical," and mainstream and alternative sites. In all four contexts she found that power relations were constantly in evidence. Power, however, was not "held" by individuals but did indeed "circulate," as Foucault suggested. Gore offers two findings that are relevant in the present context. First, she concludes that power is not something one can "get rid of" in the classroom. It is a constant. As she notes, "power relations are inescapable in pedagogy" (1994, p. 6). Second, while power is a constant, it is not exercised exclusively by the teacher upon the students; rather, power is like discourse, requiring ongoing participation and negotiation by all concerned. Both of these conclusions fly in the face of the vision of power articulated by critical pedagogy, but they support our own contentions regarding the nature of power in education.

We also want to raise a final objection to critical pedagogy, which will lead us back to our central concern of the moral dimension of teaching. Critical pedagogists believe that education is first and foremost about power and power relations; while most critical pedagogists would acknowledge that these relations have a moral component, they see power as being the crucial part in the equation—or, to use a different metaphor, as the hub of the wheel. McLaren (1989), for example, talks of "the centrality of politics and power in our understanding of how schools work" (p. 159).

Our view is that teaching in educational contexts is fundamentally concerned with moral relations, not with power. Although power relations clearly play a major part, the essence of teaching is moral in nature. This logically implies that power relations are themselves profoundly moral. The rest of this chapter will be devoted to an investigation of the ways in which this is so. We begin this examination with a look at the concept of authority, which captures the intimate connection between power and morality in schools and classrooms.

THE DUAL NATURE OF AUTHORITY IN TEACHING

Educational writers from Peters (1966) to Oyler (1996) have pointed to the double meaning inherent in the word *authority* in English (and other languages). It means the institutional power vested in the teacher to tell students what to do; and it also refers to the teacher's expert knowledge in the subject she teaches. Peters (1966) distinguishes these two meanings by talking about the teacher being *in* authority versus the teacher being *an* authority. Oyler (1996) talks in terms of "authority as process" and "authority as content." This double meaning is not accidental. Rather, it alerts us to the profound link between power and morality in teaching.

The former meaning of authority is perhaps what we more readily think of as the teacher's "power" or "authority": her ability to get children to do things, to punish and reward, to organize, and to control (Nyberg & Farber, 1986; Sennett, 1980). We will return to this understanding of authority when we look at issues such as the control of bodies. Yet the second meaning—the teacher as content-area expert—also plays a crucial role, and it is worth considering separately for a moment.

It is very much in this sense that writers such as Apple (1982) and the authors in Young (1971) use the term *power* in relation to education. They are concerned above all with the ways in which schools operate to pass on legitimated—that is, authorized—forms of knowledge. As Bourdieu (1971) puts it: "The school is required to perpetuate and transmit the capital of consecrated cultural signs, that is, the culture handed down to it by the intellectual creators of the past" (p. 178); the educational system, then, is "specially contrived to conserve, transmit and inculcate the cultural canons of a society" (p. 178).

This brings us directly to Edwards and Mercer's notion of the teacher's dilemma (1987): How can teachers get children to discover for themselves what has been planned for them in advance to learn? This is a moral question; yet it is also a question of power, not just in the sense of the imposition inherent in the word "get," but also in the sense that the very task of, consciously or otherwise, planning what children are to learn (and thus selecting which knowledge is valid and legitimate and which is not) is a process of assigning value to various forms of knowledge, and thus involves moral choice. Which works of literature should children study, for example? Which historical events should the syllabus highlight? What should students learn about other countries and peoples, and how? As we will see in chapter 4, all of these questions are profoundly moral in nature. Furthermore, so-called child-centered pedagogies, which lead teachers to devise activities whereby students discover information for themselves, still predominantly treat teachers not only as organizers but also as primary sources for deciding which knowledge is going to be discovered. In other words, teachers have moral authority by the very nature of the knowledge they have and by being sanctioned by society to "pass along" their knowledge to the young. However, for that knowledge to be "acquired" by children, it is necessary for the teacher to be *in* authority as well as *an* authority.

Our main point here is that the two dimensions of teacher authority are intimately and crucially related. In moral terms, it is the content authority of the teacher and the system in which she works that provides the moral justification for the process authority invested in her by society. Conversely, it is through authority-as-process that the legitimated forms of knowledge continue to be legitimated. Thus, power is bound up with both kinds of authority.

This close, reciprocal relation between the two kinds of authority can be seen in Bernstein's (1990, 1996) notion of pedagogic discourse, which (as we described in chapter 2) combines the two components of regulatory discourse and instructional discourse—the former referring to the teacher's role as being *in* authority, the latter to her role as *an* authority. Bernstein himself points out both the way these two discourses are inextricably combined into a single pedagogic discourse and also the fundamentally moral significance of the latter. The same relationship is reflected in Foucault's (1980) concept of *power/knowledge*. Like Bernstein, Foucault argues that legitimated forms of knowledge and legitimated forms of power are essentially part of the same regulatory mechanism. Finally, the same relationship, between the "instrumental" function of rules and the moral meaning they encode, is reflected in Boostrom's (1991) argument for a view of rules as "the embodiment of a way of life in the classroom" (p. 198).

Hoskin (1990) follows this up by drawing attention (p. 30) to another double meaning in education: that of the word *discipline*, which refers to the formal exercise of regulatory power (put simply, managing a class) and simultaneously to the legitimated bodies of knowledge that form the substance of education (the lesson that is taught). Hoskin also analyzes the way in which the two components of the power/knowledge construct are united in the concept of the *examination*, which both acts as controlling mechanism and serves to make explicit the forms of knowledge legitimated in (and by) the process of education. We will explore the nature of the examination in the section on assessment and evaluation.

All these diverse authors agree that power is not in itself a morally "bad" thing that we should seek to remove from classrooms; rather, power relations are an inevitable and inescapable feature of classroom life. With this in mind, the question becomes not, "How can we get rid of power relations?" but, "How can classroom and school power relations best be understood in terms of their moral significance, and what is the influence of these power relations on moral meanings created, maintained, and negotiated in classrooms?"

In what follows, we will use the dual meaning of authority to frame the power–morality relation in the domains of assessment, control of bodies, and voice and dialogue. These domains offer some of the clearest examples of the ways in which moral issues permeate power relations in educational settings. Yet our broader claim is that *all* matters of power in education are colored by complex moral meanings, and therefore such analyses could be performed on many other areas involving power, including gate-keeping procedures like placement testing and interviewing, streaming, forms of sanctions and punishment, and the very selection and presentation of curricular subject matter.

ASSESSMENT: EVALUATING STUDENTS THROUGH GRADING AND EXAMINATIONS

The twin roles of authority—and thus of moral meaning—can be seen to coexist in all aspects of evaluation and assessment. They are especially visible in practices such as examinations; but moral significance can also be read into alternative forms of assessment, such as self-assessment, portfolios, and even situations in which no assessment is employed. In the latter case, for instance, it could be argued that an absence of assessment practices may send a moral message about the teacher's indifference to the student's level of participation or achievement. In any case, any kind of evaluation and assessment practice conveys complex moral meanings. In the present section we will concentrate on two areas—grading and "traditional" examination practices—but our assumption is that similar analyses could be conducted on other forms of assessment.

Grading

Whenever I (Bill) have to grade students' assignments, or their achievement in a whole course, it hurts when I give a student a grade less than A. Even an A– stings. Every time I do this, I wrestle with the same arguments: To give an A to a student who has performed less well would detract from the accomplishment of the student who has achieved much greater things; furthermore, my de facto allegiance to the educational system as a whole requires my truthfulness in reporting levels of attainment. On the other hand, a grade of B or C is sending to the student a message in a voice I am reluctant to acknowledge as my own: a message that says, summarily, your performance is inferior, and this fact is to be marked for all time on your educational record.

There are further considerations, too. For a student who is not particularly strong but has made good progress and is trying hard, an A might have a strong motivating effect ("I *am* capable of getting a top grade!"); though, by the same token, the objectively superior performance of the outstanding student, also rewarded with an A, is thereby devalued. Conversely, unacceptable performance can be indicated with a lower grade—a student who has done good written work but has been absent a lot or has been "goofing off" in class might be given a B or a C; yet in such cases there is always a strong suspicion that the bad grade is being used to punish the student, not simply as a neutral indication of the student's performance.

The act of grading, then, is a moral one *par excellence*; yet it is also one in which the teacher's authority, however masked in the course of classes, reveals itself in all its glory. Nel Noddings ponders these same issues in her reflections on grading in terms of the caring relation (which, as we saw in chapter 1, is a moral relation) between the teacher as one-caring and the student as the cared-for (1984, pp. 193–196). Noddings's basic position, that relation should be central and that therefore "[t]he student is infinitely more important than the subject"

(p. 20), leads her to suggest alternatives to, or at least "ways around," the summative allotment of grades. These ways include using grades in a formative fashion to indicate progress made so far, or using a "contract method" (p. 194) based more on quantity than on quality.

Noddings's suggestions are useful, and we have drawn on them ourselves (even before we read her book) in our own teaching, in our efforts to be fair and to put the student above the content (that is, to regard the learning of individual students as more important than "covering the material" at any cost). Yet we must also acknowledge the fact that, in the real world, in the complex administrative and bureaucratic hierarchies in which we as teachers usually work, the teacher generally has limited room for maneuver in handling grades. In the real world, the moral issues surrounding grading are often too complex to unravel in their entirety.

An interesting case study of grading and its associated problems is presented by Placier (1996). Placier frames her paper as an action research study in the mold of Whitehead (1993), whose approach itself has an interesting moral foundation, insofar as the impetus for the research (and hence the action) comes from a perceived problem not of a technical nature, as often happens in action research, but one which took the form of a "contradiction" in which "my educational values are denied in my practice" (Placier, 1996, p. 25; see chapter 5 for a more extended discussion of Whitehead's work and the moral dimension of teacher development). For Placier, the contradiction lay in her grading policies and practices. As she explains, she values fairness and democracy, yet students had complained in course evaluations that grading was unfair, while she herself felt that grading as she practiced it was undemocratic—that is, decisions lay in the hands of the teacher alone, and the students were "powerless and resentful" (p. 25).

While teaching a 300-level Sociology of Education class, Placier attempted to "democratize" the grading policy by including students in the process of making decisions about how the course and its various component requirements would be evaluated. This was achieved through in-class negotiations and written responses to questions about grading and alternative forms of assessment, which were incorporated into a midterm exam (see below for a more extended discussion of the moral significance of midterms themselves). Placier reports that she was able to negotiate certain aspects of the grading system with her students—the allotment of scores to grades and the inclusion of an oral examination option—though this came at the cost of over-lengthy classroom discussions and much disagreement. Her student evaluations improved (though not in the area of "use of class time"), and she reports better teacher–student relations.

Placier's inquiry is interesting not just for itself, but also because it throws up some facts and ideas about grades and grading that cannot be ignored in a consideration of the moral significance of grading and other forms of evaluation. While her work concerns specifically grading in higher education, we can think of no fundamental reason why these ideas should not apply to other educational settings, including K–12 schooling. First, like Noddings (1984, p. 194), Placier points out that "grades have served administrative rather than pedagogical functions in higher education, as gatekeeping devices" (Placier, 1996, p. 23). Second, the system produces what Milton, Pollio, and Eison (1986) call "grade-oriented students," who "view the college experience as a crucible in which they are tested and graded and which is endured as a necessary evil on the way to getting a degree or becoming certified in a profession" (p. 126). Such students are contrasted with learning-oriented students, who see education as an end in itself and an intrinsically valuable experience.

It would seem obvious that grade-orientation is inimical to genuine learning in educational contexts, and is an extremely clear indication of the moral consequences of the exercise of power and control in the classroom. Noddings expresses this clearly in terms of the relation between teacher and student, when she describes how the teacher is immersed in this relationship, then "suddenly, grindingly, she must wrench herself from the relationship and make her student into an object of scrutiny" (Noddings, 1984, p. 195). She also talks of grading as an "intrusion" on this relation (p. 194), and says that it is "demeaning and distracting" and "violates the relationship" (p. 195). It was precisely this dilemma that Placier (1996) describes as the "contradiction" in her teaching that led her to conduct the action research project she reports in her paper.

A particularly obvious way in which grading has moral significance is the notion of the grading curve. Though not all teachers use this, many are required to, and others believe it to be a useful device. The moral consequences of the grading curve, however, must also be faced. These include the fact that, in a class in which a curve is used, some students *must* fail and others *must* get low grades. It is also arguable that this form of ranking students—against their classmates—can be more insidious than the use of national or statewide norms: The students against whom you are being evaluated are the very people sitting next to you in class; the proof of your own inferiority is not some faceless genius in the next town or state, but people whom you must deal with on a day-to-day basis and whom you may even have helped with their assignments.

Grading is a particularly stark instance of the use of power to regulate, categorize, and legitimate students—that is, to pass judgment in a variety of ways. Grading and practices like it have moral value, send moral messages to students, and provoke moral responses from those students. By grading, teachers are standing in judgment over students; and judgment, as we have shown in numerous instances, is a fundamentally moral concept.

Examinations and Testing

Examinations and related forms of testing constitute a crucial meeting point of the two dimensions of authority described above. On one hand, they revolve around the students' ability to reproduce (quite literally, onto a piece of paper) the legitimated forms of knowledge the teacher has been "teaching." On the other hand, they involve structures of coercion and control that require the institutional authority of the teacher: that is, the teacher's power to make students do and say certain things and not others (Foucault, 1977; Hoskin, 1990). Embedded in the practice of examination and testing are profound and complex moral questions that are no less important for generally being ignored.

Our basic point here is that examinations and other forms of testing send strong moral messages to students, and cause students in turn to develop and send moral messages of their own. We want to explore this topic through a particular example—the "problem" of cheating—specifically the instance of cheating that Kay Johnston found in her own class and which she describes in Johnston (1991). After summarizing the situation in Johnston's class, we offer a reanalysis of the events she narrates in light of a consideration of the moral significance of testing procedures.

Johnston describes an incident of cheating in an upper-level undergraduate class she taught on (ironically enough) moral development. Though the details are somewhat vague, it seems that during an unproctored, closed-book midterm administered in the instructor's absence, some of the students made use of their notes in ways that were not allowed. In a sensitive and probing paper, Johnston analyses her own responses to the situation, and those of her students, with whom she discussed the case openly (although without pointing fingers). She uses the twin concepts of justice and care orientations to try to understand what happened and why. She explains that the reason her sense of hurt was so great was that this act violated moral standards both from a perspective of justice—for example, in the fact that ignoring the violation or making everyone redo the test would be unfair to those students who did not cheat—and also from that of care, insofar as cheating represents an abuse of trust: "[T]hese students had broken a fundamental trust in relationship" (p. 285).

Yet what Johnston does not do is consider the moral implications of the midterm itself. She is disturbed because the incident in question provided strong evidence that the students did not feel "committed or connected" (p. 285) in her class—values she herself sought to nurture. But she seems not to consider the possibility that the very use of a midterm examination—and, further, the broader disciplinary culture of American higher education—militates against the possibility of students truly embracing values like commitment and connectedness in a college classroom.

Examinations themselves represent a colossal absence of trust. If we trusted our students—to learn, to be interested—we would not have to subject them to examinations. Instead, we regulate students—or, better still, ensure that they have regulated themselves—by obliging them to master the required, sanctioned (what Bourdieu [1971] calls "consecrated") forms of knowledge; the examination, in turn, legitimates those forms of knowledge.

The same lack of trust is apparent in the mechanisms of control common to examination rooms and halls across the country (and the world). What is proctoring but surveillance, of the same kind as that described by Foucault in his study of penality? What is the arrangement of desks in an exam hall—be it for the SAT, GRE, TOEFL, or any other kind of standardized test—but the spatial organization for purposes of control that one finds in prisons? For a person sitting in an examination room taking an SAT, Foucault's suggestive comparison between prisons and schools makes perfect sense.[1]

---

1. The practice of placing individuals under "observation" is a natural extension of a justice imbued with disciplinary methods and examination procedures. Is it surprising that the cellular prison, with its regular chronologies, forced labour, its authorities of surveillance and registration, its experts in normality, who continue and multiply the functions of the judge, should have become the modern instrument of penality? Is it surprising that prisons resemble factories, schools, barracks, hospitals, which all resemble prisons? (Foucault, 1977, pp. 227–228; see also Ball, 1990)

And, of course, as Foucault also points out (1980, p. 142), where there is control, there will also be resistance. When she interviewed her students some time after the cheating incident, Johnston was shocked to discover not only that cheating was widespread in the university but that students did not see it as an inherently bad thing. She was disturbed by this "normative student morality about cheating" (p. 287). Yet we suggest that the discourse of cheating is made possible precisely by the discourse of the midterm and of the examination system of which it is an example. Further, the fact that student attitudes to cheating seem morally charged is a direct consequence of the fact that the system of examinations that gives rise to them is also morally charged. Johnston was surprised that students did not share her view that cheating is morally problematic. But to accept the view that cheating in this context is morally wrong entails the concomitant view that the examination system itself, and the rules of conduct it insists on, are right. We submit that it is precisely a rejection of the latter—however instinctive and unconscious—that brings about the former.

And yet the story does not end here. Many teachers are familiar with the fact that, if material is not tested in some way—usually through exams or quizzes—many students will not bother to learn it. That is, quizzes provide a necessary motivation for such students. It is through exams and quizzes that they assign value to particular information and ideas. This reveals another moral dimension to assessment practices, partly reminding us of the idea mentioned above, that failure to assess also carries moral meaning—that of devaluing or disregarding the knowledge the students have acquired and, by extension (since we are evaluated, that is, assigned value, by what we know), the students themselves.

Thus, there are profound moral meanings to be read into assessment practices primarily used for the ranking of students—that is, assigning each a relative value—and for administrative purposes—that is, putting the importance of administrative convenience over that of an individual's learning processes and needs. Indeed, these meanings appear to have been read loud and clear by those students categorized as grade-oriented, and also by those who engage in cheating and who fail to see this as reprehensible.

The great majority of assessment practices, then, both involve the exercise of power and are profoundly evaluative in the broadest sense of the term. They offer a clear example of the ambiguity inherent in the terms "good student" and "bad student" (Amirault, 1995). An understanding of the interplay between morality and power in day-to-day teaching and learning must include an understanding of the power issues and moral meanings that dwell in evaluation and assessment practices.

CONTROL OF BODIES

Talk of examinations leads us to the next category of the interplay of power and morality in education: the physical control of bodies. We pointed out above that Foucault's juxtaposition of school and prison makes unnerving sense when one thinks of the conduct of public examinations. The regimenting of students does not stop here, however. It extends to the carefully aligned grid of desks in many classrooms, the intricate and strict timetables by which schooling is organized, and the rules for movement and behavior within a particular classroom. While such practices can be seen as analogs of the controlling mechanism of grades, report cards, and the like by which the student's "progress" through the system is regulated, they also constitute an important set of practices in themselves and play a vital role in the assigning of moral meanings to power relations.

In her empirical research on power in classrooms, Gore (1996) argues that "[s]urveillance, regulation and distribution may be the defining features of institutional pedagogy" (p. 6).

She further suggests that these particular techniques of power are "more corporeal: having more to do with the disciplining of bodies and conversely less connected with the learning of knowledge or content" (1996, p. 6). The latter part of this statement, in turn, implies that powerful moral messages are embedded in the exercise of this kind of power, concerning the relative values of "real" learning, control, and, ultimately, trust or the lack of it (in terms of the practice of surveillance, for example). Other writers have taken up similar themes and made similar arguments (see, e.g., Block, 1997).

We will explore the question of the control of bodies and its moral and political significance through the analysis of another piece of classroom data—in this case, an extract from a syllabus. The class in question is an English as a Second Language (ESL) lecture class at a midwestern public university. Data have been taken from Johnston, Juhász, Marken, and Ruiz (1998).

A little background is needed first. The class in question was part of an Intensive English Program (IEP), in which ESL instruction is offered to international students, many of whom plan to go on to study in American universities. The class, however, was atypical. Whereas most of the IEP's classes contained ten to fifteen students, Joe's lecture class had about fifty. It was intended as an introduction to the kind of large lecture classes many learners would face when they left the IEP to become regular university students.

Joe had taught this class in the previous session, and had run into considerable problems of organization and discipline. Attendance checks—a program requirement—were time-consuming, yet there was extensive absenteeism. Students were also often late in coming to class and failed to complete assignments. In response to these problems, Joe decided among other things to assign seats to students (the fixed seats in the auditorium where the class was held were numbered).

The following excerpt comes from the syllabus Joe presented to his class on the first day:

ATTENDANCE:
Your participation is essential for this course. Student input will be of particular importance and your attendance will be vital to your success in the course. THERE ARE NO EXCUSED ABSENCES UNLESS APPROVED BY THE INSTRUCTOR OR THE IEP PROGRAM. IF YOU ARE ABSENT MORE THAN *10* TIMES FOR THIS CLASS, YOU WILL BE GIVEN A "U" FOR THE COURSE. Each student will be assigned a seat in the classroom and he/she must sit in the given seat for attendance. If the student is not in his/her seat, he/she will be marked absent and given a "U" for participation.

Tardiness:
Please do not be late for class. If you are more than 10 minutes late to class, you will be considered absent.

This excerpt reveals many of the moral tensions inherent in the control of bodies in the classroom. Joe is a kind and friendly teacher; yet the requirement of the program to check attendance (not usually a problem in a small class) leads him in this case to create a system of assigned seating whereby he can visually keep tabs on who is present and who is not.

Whatever solution is found, Joe is faced with a series of moral dilemmas in his attempts to run the class smoothly. The present system was itself a response to the inordinate time Joe had spent on checking attendance in the previous session; thus, it is a way for him to perform a required duty at less expense of time and energy to the students and to himself. This in itself would seem a "good" thing, since it frees up everyone's attention to focus on other, more substantive things. However, the device for control he has come up with is eerily reminiscent of Bentham's Panopticon (Foucault, 1977), in which the jailer was able to keep an eye on the prisoners' doings. It also smacks of the examination hall. Neither association is one that Joe would wish to have in his classroom.

Furthermore, Joe's strict tone in the syllabus is also a response to earlier problems with attendance, homework completion, and so on. In this way, his strictness is intended to keep the learners engaged in the business of learning (in this case, English as a second language). He is "making B do something that B would not ordinarily do," and he is doing so out of a belief that the thing he is making B do is very much in B's interest. He might be said to be "saving the students from themselves." In this respect, his action can be seen as morally motivated and, many might suggest, morally justified.

Yet in this very strictness, he is also sending other moral messages of which he might be only partially aware and of which he may not approve. Two such messages seem to be particularly relevant (though there are others). First, once again there is the issue of lack of trust. In subjecting his students to these controls, Joe is sending a powerful message that he does not trust them; lack of trust, in turn, signifies a lack of belief in the underlying goodness of the other person. This belief is contrary to Joe's espoused teaching philosophy, yet it is clearly readable in his control of the students' seating.

Another important aspect of this situation is the fact that Joe is quite literally prejudging one group of students on the basis of the behavior of another. The problems he had were with an entirely different group of students; and, if we accept Noddings's (1984) argument that the moral relation is each time new and different, the contention that it is reasonable to assume that one group of students will behave like another is not only practically unsound but morally questionable. If we wished to sound melodramatic, we might say that the second group of students was being punished for the wrongdoings of its predecessors. On the other hand, of course, any practicing teacher will recognize this situation, and few would recommend treating each new group of incoming students with a clean slate.

This analysis could be extended much further. Certainly all that is said about seating applies equally to other issues, such as tardiness, homework, and so on. In all of these arrangements, teachers are exercising their power to control students' bodies and actions in ways that generally are intended to be morally justifiable but that also create unavoidable and ultimately irreconcilable moral dilemmas. Once again we are brought back to the dual character of authority: In principle, the teacher exercises her authority-as-process—the ability to create seating arrangements like Joe's, for example—in order to facilitate the students' mastery of authority-as-content. Yet, as we have suggested, both kinds of authority are linked, and both send moral messages concerning trust, relation, and belief in students. The way we control bodies in the classroom is intimately connected with the way we educate the minds contained within those bodies.

VOICE AND DIALOGUE

Evaluation practices (such as grading and examinations) and the physical manipulation of students' bodies represent clear instances of the moral significance of power relations in education. Yet moral meaning can be seen in much subtler ways that teachers have of exercising their authority. An important example of this are the ways in which voice and dialogue are handled in the classroom.

Voice is a central notion in considering the exercise and negotiation of power in the classroom. In particular, it has become a central concept for those committed to the empowerment of students (e.g., Delpit, 1988; McElroy-Johnson, 1993; Otte, 1995). It has become widely recognized that without voice—that is, roughly speaking, the power to speak (or write) out and express one's ideas and views, to "say one's mind"—students' empowerment is impossible.

As we saw in chapter 2, the third turn in the IRE sequence is the point that, in many classrooms, represents the students' best opportunity for expressing their voice; yet restrictive control of this turn by teachers leads to a nonreflexive pedagogy (Young, 1992) and to the (re)production of ritual knowledge (Edwards & Mercer, 1987).

Voice, then, is a moral as much as a political matter. To be silenced—that is, to become or be kept voiceless—is to have one's potential contribution devalued; conversely, to be able to sound one's voice is to be told that that voice is worth hearing. Once again, the way students' voices are or are not acknowledged in the classroom carries a powerful moral message.

In moral terms, the question of voice is more complex. Truly empowered students must not only have the opportunity to speak, they must be able to control when they speak; in other words, *voice* is intimately connected with *choice*. Linked to this is the option of not speaking. Power relations with a moral base must balance the right to speak with the right to be silent; only under such conditions can voice have meaning. Such a position presents a challenge to situations in which the giving of voice has become ritualized and obligatory—when, for example, the teacher goes around the circle asking students in turn for their thoughts on a given question, or even to introduce themselves and say something about themselves. Such activities do not involve voice in a morally defensible way.

Even setting this issue aside, it seems clear that voice alone is inadequate in conceptualizing the relationship between morality and power in the classroom. This fact is familiar to any teacher who has allowed students to express their interpretations of a novel or an historical event, only to worry that these interpretations are ill-formed and off base. There is a tension between what Hargreaves and Fullan (1992) call *voice* and *vision*. The former term reflects the notion of the individual's voice we have been examining here; the latter notion (vision) refers to the "accepted wisdom" that is out there, the sanctioned forms of knowledge we have found ourselves returning to time and again. This tension is a primary site of the interplay of morality and power, for it pits the moral value inherent in individual expression and respect for the views of each person with the teacher's moral imperative to educate students in ways which allow them to integrate their own knowledge with that found in the outside world. Such a dynamic revisits both Edwards and Mercer's (1987) teacher's dilemma (referred to above), and the fundamental tension of the dual nature of authority. By giving students voice, we put them *in* authority, but such a step in itself is insufficient to make them *an* authority on the subject matter at hand—it is the teacher who, for the moment at least, must retain that role.

What is needed is *dialogue*—that is, a mechanism by which individual voices (including those of sanctioned sources such as teachers and textbooks) can enter into reciprocal exchanges, learn from each other, and change organically as a result. Teaching is inherently relational in character, as educators from Freire (1972) to Noddings (1984) have long recognized; dialogue represents a process for addressing (if never fully resolving) the tension between individual voice and sanctioned forms of knowledge.

It is in dialogue that we can see the distinction between authority and authoritarianism. Authoritarianism means the dominance of a single voice—that of the teacher. Authoritarianism is monologic (Bakhtin, 1981), whereas a teacher can be an authority and still enter into dialogue with her students. A teacher's authority can inform her contribution to the dialogue, but does not dominate it. Oyler (1996), for example, describes child-led read-aloud sessions in which the children, both audience and readers, direct most of the goings-on: "Yet through all of this student-directed process, the teacher, although most often at the back of the room, remained available as an authoritative resource" (p. 85).

One indication of genuine dialogue comes when the classic teacher-centered IRE pattern of classroom discourse (e.g. Barnes, Britton, & Rosen, 1969; Cazden, 1988; Mehan, 1979) begins to break down. This is what Oyler (1996) found in the classroom she studied. Oyler reports that as she and the teacher looked at the patterns of interaction in the transcripts, "we noticed that the typical IRE pattern of teacher-controlled discourse had been displaced. What we realized is that student initiation had assumed an important place in shaping what was talked about" (p. 51). That is, students as well as the teacher were able to take the lead in classroom talk. Not only this, there was also a great variety of types of student contribution. Oyler categorized student-initiated contributions to teacher-led read-aloud sessions. These were found to include directions about process, questions, claims of expertise, references to personal experience, and sharing of affective responses (p. 53).

The moral significance of this kind of dialogue is considerable. Not only is individual voice valued, there is also a premium placed on social interaction and the negotiation of everything from classroom processes to personal meanings. Furthermore, such values as responsibility are promoted: When students know their voice is valued, listened to, and will be taken into consideration, they feel an enhanced sense of their own responsibility to participate effectively and to make sure their contribution is accurately phrased and interpreted. Put simply, they care about what they say in class, because they know it matters. It is in examples such as this that the moral dimension of empowerment through dialogue can be seen most clearly.

Yet the give and take of the tension between voice and vision present constant difficult choices to the teacher, and each time they arise they must be dealt with afresh. Likewise, dialogue is not something that can be "provided" in a one-off way, but constantly needs to be nurtured, monitored, and renegotiated. In other words, voice and dialogue are not unequivocal virtues, but rather create and exist in complex and ambiguous moral contexts in which decisions are rarely easy or straightforward. We will conclude by revisiting the beer dialogue from the previous chapter, this time to consider the power relations that underlie the negotiation of moral meaning in this activity, and the way the teacher maneuvers between vision and voice in her handling of the incident.

(1)	T:	All right, Robbie. Go ahead.
(2)	Robbie:	Okay. I'm gonna start a new ch—story, because my other one, I had so many misspelled words, and, um, I ha—, in my first chapter is at jammin' gym, and I just started on it today, and, here I go! (*Begins reading.*) Joey, come on. If we are going to jammin' gym, we have got to go now. I have rented a limo to take us there. Okay. Let's go. The limo is here. We are on our way. Joey said, "Hey guy, up in the front, where's the beer?" Under the seat. Joey, move out of the way. AAAAHH! Joe's hanging out the window. And that's all I said. (*Class claps.*) Response. (*Children put their hands up.*) Jessica.
(3)	Jessica:	How in the world did Joey get out, hanging out the window?
(4)	Robbie:	Because I pushed, I knocked him out of the way and he hit the door, and he's hanging off the door, outside, and we're going a hundred miles per hour on the freeway. He's hanging by his pinkies, and then we go up to a hundred and ten and he falls out the window. Chris?
(5)	Chris:	Um, well, this is just a suggestion, all right, um, oh, I'm just supposed to ask one question. . . . Are y'all gonna get caught drinking that beer?
(6)	Robbie:	He is. Well, actually, he's going to get arrested because he falls out the window and he rolls a couple of feet and then goes up to the bank and he goes where all the money's hid, and then he breaks in, and then he goes to jail. And then that's when the real funny part's going to be. When we go to jail. When HE goes to jail. (*To group*

		asking to see who is to share next or for a final question): Anybody? (*Students point and mumble among themselves.*) Kate.
(7)	Kate:	No. . . .
(8)	T:	Uh, before Robbie leaves I want to discuss some little something that—I'm wondering if, what you thought about. Just—when he used the word *beer* in the story, uh, I'm wondering, how do y'all feel about that?
(9)	Mark:	Some kinds of beer are good for you.
(10)	Robbie:	It's alcohol. It's nonalcohol.
(11)	Mark:	You know, like root beer, it's not alcohol.
(12)	T:	Well, that wasn't said.
(13)	Mark:	He can . . .
(14)	T:	That wasn't said, see.
(15)	Robbie:	I can change it to that.
(16)	T:	Well, I'm just thinking, you know like, uh. What would be acceptable as far as words that we use here at school? And, uh, what are your thoughts on it? (*Whispering among children: "It's okay," "I don't like it," "I don't think"; Will, standing near the teacher, says something.*)
(17)	T:	Wait a minute, turn around and tell everybody.
(18)	Will:	I don't like the wor–when he uses beer in the story. It's sort of a slang word, especially if it's a kid's story that you'll be reading to a class. I mean, grown-ups, like, if you were reading a grown-up book, you'd probably find some stuff like that in it, but not in a kid's story.
(19)	Mark:	I know, if he changed it to root beer, it'd be SAFE.
(20)	Chris:	Safe?
(21)	Ann:	I used to drink root beer. (*Robbie makes an inaudible comment.*)

(22)	Clare:	Well, what if it gets public? I mean, it'll give children the idea to do it.
(23)	Marie:	I know, and it'll influence them. (*Most students look toward the teacher.*)
(24)	T:	Okay. Well, I don't ever really want to make a person change their words or their thoughts in a story, but just every once in a while something kind of comes up, maybe a word that maybe is, might offend somebody else in the room or might, like Emily said—Emily, what was it you just said about . . . ?
(25)	Clare:	It might get published one day, and if you like . . . children . . . encourage them to do it.
(26)	T:	In other words, it might influence somebody. And again, I don't ever want to make you change something, but I just wanted to hear your thoughts on it because there's certain subjects that, uh, might or might not be acceptable to children.

The teacher's problem arises when Robbie includes beer drinking as an element in his story at (2). For the teacher, the central dilemma of morality and power seems to be roughly as follows: Her respect for the individual voices of the students—a value which, presumably, leads her to conduct such activities with the children in the first place—suggests that she should allow Robbie to write whatever kind of story he likes ("I don't ever really want to make a person change their words or their thoughts in a story," she says at [24]). However, her moral duty as Robbie's teacher is also to encourage that which is "good" and discourage that which is not; hence, this duty rather impels her to comment on his mention of beer.

This mention seems to be further prompted by at least two other considerations. First, alcohol and children are not suppose to mix in the broader society in which Robbie is being brought up (in the United States, children are generally not even allowed in liquor stores), and even more in the school community where the class takes place (many schools, for example, won't allow children to wear t-shirts with alcohol or tobacco logos). The teacher's question at (16) about whether this would be "acceptable as far as the words that we use here at school" suggests that this school may have rules of this kind. The teacher appears to think it important to emphasize this institutional and societal value.

Second, as is clear from the way the teacher involves the reactions of some of the other children, she is concerned not just about the values Robbie is "picking up" but also about the moral messages that are being sent to all the other children in the room. Yet this is complicated even further by the teacher's evident commitment to what might broadly be seen as a constructivist approach—in this case, the idea that, rather than telling children things, they are more likely to learn if they can engage their own voices in dialogue to think them through. This is why the teacher says she "just wanted to hear your thoughts on it" (26).

As a whole, the passage captures the profound moral dilemma of a teacher committed to a dialogical approach. It would be much simpler for the teacher to say something like, "I forbid you to use the word 'beer' in a story again. It's a bad word, and it doesn't belong in a third-grader's essay." It is a tribute to her teaching that she chooses a response that conveys her concern while allowing Robbie and the other children to follow the argument through by themselves. Yet it could also be said of this passage that the teacher is getting her point across just as effectively as if she *had* made the blunter statement. Indeed, it is *because* she believes this way is more effective that she employs "soft power" (Barber, 1995) rather than a heavy-handed approach. In other words, while she is not being authoritarian, she is still using her power as teacher to convey a particular moral message.

There are better and worse ways of handling such situations, but our purpose is not to pass judgment on the teacher.

Rather, we want to argue that these situations can be best conceptualized in terms of the tensions of morality and power that are unavoidably inherent in them. As explained in chapter 2, Bernstein's notion of pedagogic discourse, which comprises by definition the twin components of regulative discourse and instructional discourse, perhaps best captures this dynamic between moral and political forces in the classroom. The tensions between power and morality can never be resolved; however, they can be explored and better understood.

CONCLUSION

The three areas of teaching examined above are intended not as an exhaustive account of the relationship between power and morality in the classroom, but as indicators of how pervasive this relationship is in the processes of education. We offer these analyses as evidence of our claim that this relation in fact enters into all aspects of teaching and learning. For any teacher who accepts the centrality of both power relations and moral issues in teaching, the relation between them should be a source of continual reflection. This is so not only because of its importance but because, as we have seen, context plays a vital role, and the complex, changing nature of each particular classroom and each group of learners means that the relationship between power and morality must constantly be reevaluated and reconceptualized.

Complex as the relationship between power and morality is, however, it does not give us a full picture of the moral dimensions of the classroom. As we saw in chapter 2, questions of language factor into the equation, too. All of these value-laden features are further complicated by the question of culture and by the image of the classroom as the meeting ground of different and possibly conflicting sets of cultural values. It is to this that we turn in the next chapter.

FOUR

Participation, Representation, and Identification

Culture and Morality in Classrooms

INTRODUCTION

Culture has become a central notion in education, both in the United States and elsewhere. Research over the last few decades has shown convincingly how the cultural expectations that children bring from home and community environments are often significantly different from those they encounter at school. These expectations include everything from eye contact and the importance of working individually versus collaboratively, to the content of history and social science books. Furthermore, it has been shown that, even though this is so, much that goes on in education continues to assume that all children hold the same expectations. The net result is that children from nonmajority cultural backgrounds—whether African American, Native American, Hispanic, or immigrant and refugee populations—fail at school disproportionately in relation to white, middle-class children.

Our main goal in this chapter is to consider the moral dimension of cultural contact in the classroom. We acknowledge the huge role of culture in education (and beyond, of course), and we assume that our readers are already familiar with this phenomenon. Here we want to uncover and analyze

80

the *moral* significance of the existence of cultural differences in the classroom. In the process of this analysis, we will revisit and integrate much of what was said earlier about the importance of language and power in the workings of the moral dimensions of classroom interaction. As elsewhere in the book, our central goal is to focus on the realities of classroom interaction in which different cultural values come into contact.

Our understanding of culture comprises two fundamental components. First, we see culture as fundamentally a question of values—that is, of moral judgments. We will assume axiomatically (rather than argue) that culture is primarily a closely interrelated set of moral standpoints, and that other trappings of culture—history, customs, celebrations, clothing, food, and so on—are only secondary manifestations of the core values of the culture. Thus, culture is, above all else, a moral matter.

Second, we follow recent scholarship on culture (e.g., Holland, Lachicotte, Skinner, & Cain, 1998; Strauss & Quinn, 1997) in conceiving of culture not as an impersonal force but as a set of linguistic, discursive, and other resources for understanding and acting upon the world. By this understanding, culture is both cognitive (i.e., individual) and social; culture constrains people's behavior and cognitions but does not absolutely determine them, because there is always room for individual agency. This model of culture, then, mirrors our view of morality (and also of language and of power) as something both individual and social in nature, which takes its essence neither from one thing nor from the other but from the complex interplay between the two.

Our own view of the place of culture in education is that its importance has been both understated and overstated. The importance of culture has been understated because the kinds of values an individual takes from culture are often profound and also so deeply embedded as to be unreachable, for better or worse. These values are also often subconscious—neither the bearer of the values nor the outsider can quite put a finger on what it is about. The attempts of disciplines such as cross-cultural communication have tended to simplify the situation by presenting cultural beliefs and values more as a semiotic code and by suggesting that in "cracking the code" we "understand the culture." While not denying the obvious importance of the signals of cultural values, we believe the values themselves can be approached only from a moral standpoint, in which they are seen in terms of what is right and wrong, good and bad. This is a much harder way of thinking about cultural values, but it is essential in understanding how inextricably they are linked with individuals.

Another aspect of current approaches to cultural matters in education that has underestimated their significance is the somewhat blinkered view of cultures represented in "multiculturalism." Multicultural materials, although of undoubted benefit, have often ignored the true diversity of American classrooms and have focused rather on established minorities such as African-American, Chinese-American, or Mexican-American learners. Without in the least wanting to disparage these groups, let us just point out that—especially at a time when immigration is again on the increase yet is being drawn from different countries than in the past, and when ESL students constitute a growing percentage of children in classrooms, dramatically so in some urban settings[1]—the true nature of multiculturalism is much richer. Depending on where one works, one might see classrooms with large numbers of Somali, or Russian, or Iraqi children alongside the "traditional" immigrant groups from Mexico and Vietnam; there may be children from Romania, the Ukraine, Ethiopia, Haiti, or the Philippines (García, 1999; Rong & Preissle, 1998). These newer immigrants are largely ignored in discussions of multicultural-

---

1. García (1999), for example, reports that the 1980s saw a sixty-three percent increase in immigration over the previous decade, while the increase continued into the 1990s (pp. 12–14). In Indiana, the number of Limited English Proficient (LEP, another term for ESL) students has risen from around 4,000 in 1990 to more than 13,000 in 2000. Similar or even more dramatic figures have been reported from most U.S. states.

ism. We understand that part of the reason for this is that the very notion of multiculturalism itself is under siege (Ovando & McLaren, 2000) and that in many contexts it is fighting a retrograde battle; nevertheless, a significant percentage of children remain largely unrepresented. For this reason, too, the place of culture in American classrooms has been understated.

On the other hand, the importance of cultural values has been overstated. Looking at the study of culture over the past few decades, a different story might be told. According to this story, the notion of culture has been reified, one might even say fetishized, in education, the social sciences, and the humanities. Once the importance of culture in understanding human behavior and beliefs was revealed in the early writings of anthropology, cross-cultural communication, ethnographies of schooling, and so on, it was as if no other force existed. Children in schools, members of communities, and characters in novels came to be identified primarily in cultural terms—as white, black, Asian American, or Native American, to give examples from the U.S. context. The term *culture* came to refer to an impersonal force compelling each of us to act in particular ways because of our ethnicity, national origins, or upbringing.

We do not deny the influence culture has on the individual, nor do we want to downplay the ways in which cultural differences were for many decades swept under the mat (and in many contexts continue to be), but ultimately the current view of culture is one-sided and also does injustice to children and others who are seen in such terms. One of the central points in this chapter is the idea that individual values play as much of a role in moral interaction as do cultural values. The simple fact is that no individual is a "perfect" representative of his or her culture. Indeed, in many cases individuals find themselves either consciously or unwittingly pitted against values associated with their own society (see, for example, the expatriate American teachers working in Japan studied by Duff and Uchida [1997]). In such cases, individuals find themselves espousing values that are foreign, even hostile, to prevalent values in their own society.

This is not to deny that they still carry internalized values from that culture, but in no single instance is the set of values enshrined in a culture coextensive with those of any individual. Even this view represents a grossly oversimplistic understanding of culture. Most so-called cultures in the real world are themselves dynamic and filled with contradictions and debate; furthermore, as MacCannell (1992) and many others have pointed out, the very notion of an idealized, single, free-standing culture is itself an illusion, as cultures necessarily exist side by side, in contact, and are continually influenced by one another. This has always been the way of things.

In this chapter, we will look at three aspects of interaction in classrooms. First, we will reconsider the notion of classroom discourse from a cultural point of view. How are moral values instantiated in the moves and negotiations of discourse in the classroom? What is the moral dimension of culturally influenced patterns of interaction? And what moral meanings exist in the ways minority children are or are not able to take part in the cultural life of the classroom? This section will focus in particular on the notion of *participation*. Second, we will look more broadly at the role played by curriculum and materials in classroom work, and especially at the issue of *representation* and its moral foundations. Third and last, we will examine the issue of identity and *identification*, asking questions such as these: Who do we become through our schooling? How is this identity related to, or separate from, other cultural identities we consciously or unconsciously claim? How does it relate to identities that are assigned to us by others? What is the moral dimension of the processes of cultural and individual identity formation in schooling? In pursuing our investigations, we will revisit and attempt to integrate themes and ideas from previous chapters.

CULTURE AND PARTICIPATION IN THE CLASSROOM

The issue we will look at first is participation. By this we mean both participation in the narrow sense of taking part in class discussions and other interactions, and in the broader sense of being a member of the school community. Of course, both kinds of participation are influenced by individual differences among children. Yet it is also true that certain aspects of culture impact the extent and the nature of a child's participation both in day-to-day classroom discourse and in the broader processes of education. It is these aspects of culture—and, more specifically, their moral significance—that we will discuss in the present section.

Participation and Language

Perhaps the single most crucial thing children need in order to participate in classroom and school interaction is language: both generally speaking the language of the community (English, in the case of the United States) and specifically, the language of academic work. As Heath (1983) and others have shown with great clarity, minority children find themselves at a disadvantage in both areas.

It is hard for most Americans to appreciate the incredible task faced by someone, whether child or adult, who is forced to begin schooling in a completely unknown language, and is aware that nothing short of absolute mastery of that language will suffice. Learning a new language involves mastering a complex, irregular, and often irrational grammar; a bizarre and difficult set of new sounds; a new semantics; and new discourse and pragmatic conventions. It is perhaps one of the hardest things children have to do in schools.

Above all, from a moral point of view, learning a new language entails building new relationships, and doing so upon ground that is uncertain. We have already seen how language is a fundamental component of the moral relation. If we consider the vagaries of using a second language—the possibilities for misunderstanding at every level, from the syntactic and the phonological to that of differing discourse conventions and pragmatics in the first and second languages—the potential hindrances to developing relations (with teachers and with classmates) are formidable. Witness the following exchange from Grugeon and Woods (1990, p. 41). Abbas is a five-year-old Urdu speaker in the reception class of a British inner-city school; he comes from an Islamic family from an unspecified South Asian country. In this extract, which was recorded in week ten of his first term, he struggles to convey some personal information to the teacher:

Mrs. Smith:	Abbas—going to London?
Abbas:	I no com aschool.
Mrs. Smith:	You're not coming swimming? Why not?
Abbas:	No, I no com aschool.
Mrs. Smith:	You're not coming to school. When?
Abbas:	I a go London.
Mrs. Smith:	You're going to London. What are you going to see?
Abbas:	Toys.
Mrs. Smith:	Some toys in London. What sort of toys? (*Abbas made a huge gesture indicative of something very large.*)
Simon:	He's going to see big toys.
Mrs Smith:	He's going to see big toys in London.
Abbas:	Es gooderbye, goodbye. [. . .]
Mrs. Smith:	Goodbye?
Abbas:	No, a scooter. A scooter bike. (*He enunciates this carefully.*)
Mrs. Smith:	A scooter bike.
Abbas:	I, a scooter bike, I have one.
Mrs. Smith:	You've got one.
Abbas:	No.
Mrs. Smith:	You're going to get one?
Abbas:	I go in London, das too big.
Mrs. Smith:	I see yes. You're going with your dad?
Abbas:	Mm.
Mrs. Smith:	And your mum?
Abbas:	Kafief. (*His intonation indicates* and *Kafief.*)

Mrs. Smith: Kafief.

What stands out above all else in this extract is the extraordinarily powerful drive that Abbas evinces to share personal information with the teacher. This exchange is extremely labored and riddled with misunderstandings that have to be cleared up equally laboriously, one by one; but Abbas perseveres. Morally speaking, he is riding roughshod over the forms of the language in order to achieve the goal of establishing relation with the teacher. The teacher, in her own way, is doing the same. The extract illustrates, then, both the immense difficulty this process presents and the powerful need felt by both child and teacher to see it through. Take, for example, the initially paradoxical exchange:

Abbas: I, a scooter bike, I have one.
Mrs. Smith: You've got one.
Abbas: No.

At first sight, it seems to the reader—and to Mrs. Smith—that Abbas is saying he has a scooter bike. If this were the case, his response "No" would seem to make no sense. What he is actually saying, of course, is that he is *going to have* one—a grammatical form that is beyond his current level of ability. Both teacher and child have to struggle further before the information is accurately conveyed. (Exchanges of this kind, by the way, are repeated every day in ESL and EFL [English as a Foreign Language] classrooms everywhere.) To downplay the magnitude of this feat is to dismiss an act of moral courage on the part of the child and the teacher. The moral act of the teacher can be seen as a willingness to engage in the effort. The teacher becomes vulnerable, in this case allowing herself to feel "stupid" because she risks having to learn a new language rather than forcing the child to learn her language. Thus, she is willing to meet the child halfway.

The ability to maintain a conversation, however, is not even half the story. It is a well-established fact in the study of second language acquisition (SLA) that children are capable relatively quickly (say, within a year or two, sometimes even less) of reaching a point at which they can take part in heavily contextualized, face-to-face interaction—in which, for example, using words such as "this" or "that" and gestures can overcome lack of vocabulary or syntactic competence (Gibbons, 1998). However, it takes much, much longer for the same children to master the decontextualized, formal, mostly written language of academic work. Cummins (1980) has labeled these two kinds of knowing language Basic Interpersonal Communication Skills (BICS) and Cognitive Academic Language Proficiency (CALP). He estimates that whereas BICS can be acquired in a relatively short time, CALP can take up to *seven years or longer* to master. And until CALP is acquired, children's ability to learn through English is impaired.

The moral consequences of these facts are huge. Teachers and administrators are faced with a series of major moral dilemmas. Should standards for work done by LEP children be lowered to allow them to succeed? How much time should be spent teaching the language and how much on subject matter knowledge? Should funds be spent on bilingual education or on providing increased ESL support? This whole issue, of course, is highly politicized. Two facts, however, must be acknowledged. First, there is a vast amount of research demonstrating that, just because a child appears to be able to maintain a conversation in English, this does not mean he or she has mastered academic English. Second, whatever one's political beliefs, the moral dilemmas concerning the education of LEP children remain: If one is concerned about these children being given equal opportunities, one must be able to envisage alternative forms of support for them.

Participation in Classroom Discourse

There is a narrow sense of "participation" that simply means taking part in class activities. Even this kind of participation, though, is rife with potential cultural mismatches and misunderstandings; nor does a knowledge of English necessarily equip students for it. Certain cultures have a preference for (and thus socialize their children into) communal, collaborative approaches to problem solving rather than the individualism preferred (often exclusively) in mainstream classrooms; this preference has been claimed, for example, for African-American culture and for Native-American cultures (Philips, 1983), and is also true of many cultures from outside the United States. This preference considerably impedes the ability of young children to succeed in school, where value is placed overwhelmingly upon individual work and individual achievement (and, as we have said, anything that carries value is moral in nature).

A related cultural issue is that of active participation in the form of asking questions, volunteering answers, and making contributions to discussions. Of course, children's participation in these ways is affected by personality (whether they are shy or outgoing, for example), but it is also the case that their previous cultural experiences may have a powerful impact. Many immigrant children, for example, come to the United States after years of very traditional, formal education in which teachers are to be listened to and in which it is seen as insolent and disrespectful for a child to speak without being spoken to, let alone to disagree with a teacher. We have encountered this frequently with international graduate students; how much more awkward, then, must disempowered young children feel in such situations? Yet another related cultural difference is the oft-mentioned matter of eye contact and gaze: Many teachers complain that children "will not look them in the eye," but in many cultures such eye contact between a higher status teacher and a lower status student is frowned upon, and the avoidance of eye contact is simply an indication of respect.

One well-documented culturally influenced aspect of classroom participation is the African-American "topic-associated" style of story telling, which entails "a series of implicitly associated anecdotal segments, with no explicit statement of an overall theme or point" (Michaels, 1981, p. 221; cited in Davis & Golden, 1994, p. 268). An example of this appears in Gallas (1998), who describes stories told by an African-American child called Germaine. Germaine's stories "seemed disjointed in their development, jumping from one scenario to another" (p. 91). Gallas says they were "not linear stories, beginning with a problem and then proceeding logically toward the problem's resolution, but were rather what I would call circular stories, creating intertextual relationships among many other aspects of his own and the other children's lives" (p. 91). Gallas emphasizes that the stories "were always compelling because he included his classmates as central characters" (p. 91). While Gallas is capable of appreciating the stories for what they were, it is certain many other teachers would be more like the two white teachers studied by Davis and Golden (1994), who said that some (minority) students' "thought processes are all cobwebby in there" (p. 275).

What are the moral implications of these cultural influences on the nature of children's participation in class? At least three major issues arise. First, as pointed out above, the preferred patterns of interaction in classrooms are not merely conventions but have *value* attached to them—that is, above all else, they carry moral weight. Looking at the teacher, working on one's own, or telling stories in what is perceived by the teacher to be a coherent manner—all of these are value-laden forms of interaction. Children learning to follow such norms are being taught moral values; they are also being implicitly taught moral values for the opposite behaviors, a fact that reveals areas of moral conflict between home and school environments.

Second, these behaviors critically impede the development of the moral relation between teacher and child, which is the linchpin of the educational enterprise. A child who acts in ways the teacher cannot understand or, worse, misinterprets as rudeness or incompetence is going to find it much harder to develop a relation with that teacher. The teacher unfamiliar with the student's cultural norms for interaction will, to paraphrase Noddings, find it much harder to see the student's reality as a possibility for her own (Noddings, 1984, p. 14). Given the crucial role of discourse in establishing and maintaining the moral relation (see chapter 2), in cases where the two sides are playing by different discursive rules, the nature of that moral relationship is in grave danger because of serious misunderstandings and miscommunications.

Third, and perhaps most important, children's failure to adopt mainstream norms for classroom interaction sets them up for failure in school; and this is the ultimate moral judgment passed on a child—that he or she is not worth as much as the other children. For many minority children, there is an intimate link between being "bad" students in the sense of not behaving like students are supposed to behave (maintaining eye contact with the teacher, doing one's own work), and subsequently becoming "bad" students in terms of performance in school (McCadden, 1998). We will explore this matter further in the section on the identities constructed for minority children in school settings.

Participation and Belonging

Yet there is also a broader way in which children participate in school. This participation comes above all from a sense of belonging—of sharing the same cultural experiences, points of reference, and values as those around you. In these ways, too, children from non-mainstream homes are often at a disadvantage. We were struck by a very simple yet telling passage in which Gallas (1998) introduces the background of Germaine, the African-American child described above:

> Germaine was from a working-class family with ten children living in the house. Both parents worked long hours, and Germaine was cared for by a variety of older siblings, aunts,

and uncles. Germaine did not have a lot of toys and books; his family did not own a computer; he did not routinely watch videos. He had not attended kindergarten at our school and had not gone to preschool. His weekends were filled with visits to and from his large extended family, pick-up basketball and football games, and the communal mak-ing of meals. If he interacted with his classmates outside of school, it was during a soccer practice, or the result of a chance meeting in the park. (pp. 86–87)

What struck us about this passage was simply how different Germaine's life experiences were from those of his white class-mates. This is not in the least to suggest that in absolute terms it is worse; quite the opposite, visiting with extended family and making meals together seems a rather superior way of spending time to watching videos. Yet, from Germaine's point of view, he is different from the other children in the class; and from the child's perspective, this can be the crucial point. A child who does not watch videos lacks points of cultural ref-erence in interacting with other children; in Bourdieu's (1991) terms, Germaine lacks *cultural capital*. This is an experience familiar to all immigrants to the United States: Casual cultural references in daily conversation are incomprehensible. Nor-ton Peirce (1995) recounts a story told by one of her infor-mants, an adult female immigrant to Canada from Poland, about the embarrassment she experienced when it came out in conversation that she did not know who Bart Simpson was:

"Don't you know him?"
  "No. I don't know him."
  "How come you don't know him. Don't you watch TV. That's Bart Simpson."
  It made me feel so bad and I didn't answer her nothing. Until now I don't know why this person was important. (p. 10)

Speaking a shared cultural language is not only useful in building friendships with other children, it also plays a key role in the development of the child's relations with the teacher. The white teachers in Davis and Golden's study (1994), for example, complained that the African-American children lacked basic concepts like names for meals and generally the idea of a daily schedule—that their daily routine was "all scrambled up" (p. 274). Davis and Golden point out correctly that "judging children's behavior according to [one's] own (mainstream) values results in failure to consider alternative possibilities, such as variation in use of terms and ways in which to schedule everyday life within socioculturally different communities" (p. 275). What we are left with is a profound mismatch between the life experiences of the teacher and those of the learner; thus, the children's participation extends to their ability (or otherwise) to take part in the sociocultural context in which the classroom is situated as well as the day-to-day interactions within it. The moral significance of this, in turn, is clear. Like the issues of classroom participation discussed above, the failure to establish commonalities of cultural reference hinders the establishment and growth of the moral relation between student and teacher through shared dialogue, as well as making it more difficult for the child to become a member of his or her peer group in games and so on. It also reveals the way in which certain cultural experiences are assigned greater value than others. For Germaine, in the home setting family get-togethers carry moral value; yet at school, at least with his peers, greater value is given to fluency with popular culture and its referents. Thus, Germaine finds himself uncomfortably at the nexus of conflicting cultural values.

Participation as Contribution

Along with cultural capital and mastery of the dominant language and its academic discourses, a final aspect of participation children need in order to participate fully in the classroom is recognition of what they themselves bring to the processes and content of schooling. The disproportionate failure of minority children was once explained by the theory of cultural deficiency, which argued that such children lack cultural knowledge and abilities that mainstream children possess. This theory has since been thoroughly discredited in educational research circles, with the growing realization that children's home languages and cultures are equally valid to, just different from, those of the mainstream. However, this message has not always been heard by teachers, many of whom continue, consciously or unconsciously, to assume a deficit explanation of cultural differences in the classroom (see, e.g., Davis & Golden, 1994). Authors such as Kenner (1999) have demonstrated that even very young minority children (she looks at three- and four-year-olds in a British nursery school) bring rich multicultural and multilingual experiences of literacy to class and, when given the opportunity, are able to make creative use of these experiences in moving toward literacy, often in two or more languages. Yet these experiences are often not acknowledged in the classroom. Kenner states: "There needs to be greater recognition amongst educators that children are developing understandings of genre from a very early age, both in English and in other languages. These understandings need to be acknowledged and called upon within the classroom" (pp. 12–13).

The "invisibility" of what minority children bring to school is linked to the cultural hegemony that exists in many multicultural educational settings. Even in ostensibly multicultural and bilingual contexts, English dominates over other languages—that is, in moral terms, it is assigned greater value. Shannon (1995) describes the hegemony of English in American bilingual education, in which Spanish frequently is "the inferior language" (p. 183), and resistance to this assignment of values in a fourth-grade bilingual class. Martin-Jones and Saxena (1996) describe classroom interactions with low-status bilingual teaching assistants in a British primary school reception class; they demonstrate how these Panjabi- and Urdu-speaking teachers were discursively positioned as "marginal to the main action of the class," and how "the bilingual resources they brought to the classes were contained within a primarily monolingual order of discourse" (p. 121). Many theoretical studies have examined the notion of hegemony; we cite these studies because they focus on empirical classroom discourse and show how hegemonic linguistic relations are played out in the everyday interactions of the classroom. The hegemony of English, in turn, entails a failure to recognize the importance (the value, that is) of the home languages spoken by LEP children.

An example demonstrating the value of acknowledging what children bring to the class is found in Ballenger (1997). Ballenger's study looked at a science teaching program for Haitian immigrant children. In this mixed fifth- through eighth-grade class, taught by a bilingual teacher, "science talks" (Gallas, 1995), or whole-class discussions, were used to integrate children's out-of-school knowledge with the topics in question, in an effort to encourage them to ask questions themselves and to think about how to pursue answers. In the following extract (from Ballenger, 1997, pp. 5–6), Sylvio Hippolyte, the teacher, has asked the children where mold is found and under what conditions. The dialogue was originally conducted in Haitian Creole:

Manuelle:	Because they just leave stuff there, take no care, they don't clean, they just [ ] if you have a toilet in Haiti, you take care of it, it won't have mould. (*Paske yo just kite bay la yo pa pran swen yo, yo pa clean yo just [ ] so ou gen yon twalèt Ayiti, ou prean swen li li pap fe limon.*)
Sylvio:	Children, let me say something. OK, all right, she said that [her toilet] doesn't make mould. You, you said you don't agree. Explain. (*Timoun, kite m di yon bagay. [ ] OK. all right [ ], li di [ ] pa fè limon. Ou menm ou di ou pa dako. Eksplike [ ].*)

Student:	Toilets make mould! (*Twalet fe limon!*)
Manuelle:	Not all. (*E pa tout.*)
Sylvio:	How do you explain? (*Koman eksplike?*)
Student:	[ ] toilet downstairs has mould. (*[ ] twalet anba fe limon.*)
Student:	[ ] clean it. (*[ ] clean li.*)
	Manuelle then reclaims the floor.
Manuelle:	OK. What I told you, I told you, MY TOILET at MY HOUSE doesn't have mould because I CLEAN it! (*E ben, sa m dit ou la, mwen menm twalèt lakay mwen pa fè limon paske m clean li!*)
Student:	All toilets have mould. (*Tout twalèt fe limon.*)
Manuelle:	Not all! (*E pa tout!*)

From our perspective, the most interesting thing about this extract is the way the children's prior, nonschool knowledge is represented in the classroom by giving the children the space to integrate what they already know with what is being learned in school. As Ballenger points out, this discussion is very different from what is usually heard in science classrooms: The style is informal, and the content is not restricted to the "scientific" and scholarly but incorporates the personal and domestic. Yet it is precisely through this "full" representation that the children are able and willing to engage in sustained inquiry. Ballenger reports that, at the end of the unit on mold, the children not only had voluntarily learned a great deal of detail about the topic but, perhaps even more importantly, were eager to ask further questions about the subject (1997, p. 10).

Ballenger herself talks of the children's narratives as being "moral" in nature; by this she means that the children's discussions of cleanliness in their respective homes carried a strong personal and evaluative component. We would argue that the moral significance of the Haitian Creole program — and, generally speaking, of the issue of how the child's home culture is represented and acknowledged in class—goes much further. It is true of children in general that their learning is enhanced when it acknowledges and builds on the experiences, knowledge, and understandings they bring to class, rather than assuming tabula rasa. Dewey pointed this out many years ago (1938), and it is still true. With children from minority cultures, however, there is an ever-present danger that, through ignorance or worse, it will be harder for them to integrate their home experiences with their schooling. The moral consequences of a failure to do so, however, go to the heart of identity and personal worth.

To conclude, then, the notion of participation is a rich and complex one. Full participation in class means involvement in the daily interactions of the classroom; but it is also rooted in the broader life experiences of children and may depend crucially on whether these are shared. More than anything else, participation is dependent on adequate access to language, both in the general sense and in the specific languages of schooling and of the various subjects learned at school. Finally, full participation is possible only when the cultural experiences children bring to the classroom are consistently and overtly valued; their participation involves bringing things to class as well as taking them away from class.

THE MORALITY OF CULTURAL REPRESENTATION

The second aspect of culture in educational settings we will examine is that of *representation*. Our understanding of cultural representation begins with Harklau's (2000) definition of representation as "the images, archetypes, or even stereotypes of identity with which students are labeled" (p. 37). Cultural representation refers to those aspects of representation that are based on understandings of "culture." We also extend Harklau's definition to include not just institutional labels but also ways in which "other cultures" are represented in curricular materials—that is, how representations of these cultures are enshrined in the content of teaching and learning. In our discussion, then, we will focus on one kind of representation: how the cultures of minority children are represented in materials studied in classes. Such analyses have been conducted before (see, e.g., Dilg, 1999; McCarthy & Crichlow, 1993). We will propose a new perspective, however, from which to view these representations, by asking this question in each case: What is the moral significance of the way cultures are represented, misrepresented, or not represented at all by curricular materials?

Countries and ethnicities other than those of the dominant group (white, middle-class Americans) often crop up in curricular materials of one kind or another. The significance of these occurrences, however, can most clearly be seen when "representatives" of those cultures are present in the classroom and can comment on them. For this reason, we begin with three anecdotal stories of cultural representation. We will then look at some middle-school textbooks to find further examples of cultural representation.

Bill (the coauthor of this book) is married to a Polish woman; his children were brought up in Poland for the first years of their lives, and have Polish citizenship. One day his younger daughter came home from middle school complaining to her parents about how Poland had been shown in her social studies textbook—with nothing but pictures of farmers and factories. She felt the book presented an image of the country that did not convey her own experience of the country—the richness of childhood experiences (further enriched by her many visits since she came to the United States) and the warmth of family and friends. To state the case simply, she felt that her country—and, by extension, she herself—had been belittled by the representation in the book.

Her story echoes that recounted by an immigrant to the United States from Vietnam and reported in Macedo (1994). This boy tells of sitting through endless history lessons in American school about a history to which he could not relate.

At last, the subject of Vietnam came up. "I was so excited when my history teachers talked about the Vietnam War. Now at last, I thought, now we will study about my country. We didn't really study it. Just for one day, though, my country was real again" (Olsen, 1988, p. 68; cited in Macedo, 1994, p. 125). One can imagine the way this excitement was tempered by the fact that the country in question is associated almost exclusively in the popular American view with a bloody war.

The last and most dramatic story comes from an elementary school in a small, predominantly white town near a Dakota Indian reservation in Minnesota. One day during the 1998–1999 school year, a Native-American third-grader who attended the school came home deeply upset because of a passage in the book her class had been reading. The book was Laura Ingalls Wilder's *Little House on the Prairie* (1935/1981), an acknowledged classic of children's literature. The girl had been upset by a chapter in which two Indians—"two naked, wild men" (p. 134)—visit the white family's cabin uninvited. Reading the passage, it is not hard to imagine how disturbing it might be to a Native-American child (or adult, come to that):

> They were tall, thin, fierce-looking men. Their skin was brownish-red. Their heads seemed to come up to a peak, and the peak was a tuft of hair that stood straight up and ended in feathers. Their eyes were black and still and glittering, like a snake's eyes . . . "Indians!" Mary whispered. Laura was shivering and there was a queer feeling in her middle.[2] (p. 134)

Here is a clear example of the problematic nature of cultural representation. In fact, this incident prompted a case that was reported nationwide. As the children read the book the teacher had not commented on the nature of the text, thus failing to bring to the children's awareness the (mis)representation that

---

2. It's quite another matter that the Indians described by Wilder and depicted in the illustrations to the book are not those who lived in the region where the story takes place, but of another tribe. For Wilder, the generic term "Indian" was all that was needed.

was taking place; she also refused to stop using the book as a required reading. As it stands, the Wilder passage is a classic example of how, despite all the "advances" of political correctness, certain cultures continue to be represented in mainstream educational settings. It is also one of the sources of the popular mainstream images of Indians that to this day are perpetuated through literature, film, and popular culture. The net result is that a child's culture, and the child herself, was belittled and misrepresented in class.

To further probe the first of these stories (about Bill's daughter's social studies class) we took a small representative selection of recent middle-school geography textbooks to see how Poland, Poles, and Polish culture are represented. We chose this country because it is one with which Bill has first-hand experience: He lived there for eight years and maintains daily contact with the language, the people, and the culture. Poland is also a country from which there continues to be significant immigration to the United States. We wanted to see how Poland is represented to children in American classrooms. We examined four books aimed at grades seven and eight: Baerwald and Fraser (1995), Banks et al. (1995), Boehm (1997), and Boehm, Armstrong, and Hunkins (1996).

Our brief survey of these four texts showed that Bill's daughter's impression was not mistaken. The images of Poland in these texts fall almost exclusively into a few restricted categories. One category includes images of farming and agriculture, often involving "primitive" equipment and methods such as using a horse and cart rather than a tractor, or digging by hand (e.g., "A potato harvest in Poland" in Boehm et al., 1996, p. 325). Such images recur across representations of many "East European" countries[3]

---

3. The great majority of people from this part of the world refer to themselves as "Central Europeans" or simply "Europeans," and object to being categorized as "East European." Indeed, one of the books examined here (Banks et al., 1995) explicitly quotes Czech poet Jaroslav Seifert as saying: "For us, there is no eastern Europe. It is a collection of countries . . . You should not see us as a single entity" (p. 330). Despite this admonition, the book, like all the others, continues to use this label.

in the book, including Belarus and Lithuania as well as Poland. Second, there are images of heavy industry, mostly connected with environmental pollution—two books, for example, contained a picture of the Nowa Huta steel mill near Kraków, the city that Bill's wife is from and where his children were partly raised; in one of these books (Boehm, 1997), this was the only picture of Poland. Finally we found images of the kind Lutz and Collins (1993) label *exotic*—for example, a "traditional Polish wedding" in Boehm et al. (1996, p. 326; see also Baerwald & Fraser, 1995, p. 353). In the caption to this picture we are told, "Many Polish couples dress in traditional clothes on their wedding day"; this statement is misleading, as most Poles dress very much like people in the United States at weddings. Weddings of the kind shown in the picture are restricted to rural areas—for example, in the mountains of the far south, where this particular photo was taken. Such weddings are exotic for other Poles as well as for Americans, a fact not mentioned in the text.

In moral terms, the net result of the choices of image described here is a misrepresentation of Poland. Although these books are clearly trying to use the limited space available for each country to convey something of that country, they end up perpetuating stereotypical notions of Poland and Polishness. It is from texts like these—as well as from jokes, TV shows, and elsewhere—that the image of Poland as a cold, dreary, dirty, backward place originates. That this is so can be seen by applying an argument borrowed from Jackson et al. (1993), which is cited above. Jackson et al. point out that children develop a lasting impression of a teacher not from a single, dramatic act but from a multitude of small, subtle things. We want to suggest that images of countries, cultures, and people are likewise gleaned—indirectly in the great majority of cases, as most American children have not visited Poland or the other countries studied—from various sources. That Poland is not cold (at least no more than, say, Indiana), dreary, or backward can only be known by those who have spent time there and experienced the living culture(s) of the country. That Native Americans do not smell or have reptilian eyes is immediately apparent when one meets them; yet, of course, most mainstream children do not have even that opportunity.

Another way of putting this is to say plainly that the materials, in a very real and direct sense, present misinformation—that is, their truthfulness is at stake. And truthfulness, we recall, is one of the elements of the curricular substructure identified by Jackson et al. in their examination of the moral dimensions of teaching. By giving children misleading images of other countries and cultures, we are performing a morally culpable act not only with regard to the children thus represented but also toward those who are being taught about the culture as outsiders.

Of course, it is also true that the (mis)representation of Poland—with its simplifications and reductions, its exoticism, and its selectivity—is matched by misrepresentations of many other countries and peoples in these and similar materials. Certainly the other East European countries in these books fared no better. In fact, it is highly unlikely that a handful of pages could do justice to any country, culture, or ethnic group, a point to which we will return later. But if this is so and our suppositions are correct, the stories we told earlier must reflect the experiences of thousands upon thousands of children in American schools.

The point is that cultural representation is not merely a matter of presenting generalized information about huge numbers of peoples categorized in particular ways; it is also a question of reflecting the lived experience of the children in the classroom. To the extent that children's experiences are not represented, their lives—in the richest sense of the term—are not present in the classroom either. And this, as we have said, is a moral matter. Several moral aspects of cultural representation might suggest themselves, but we will look here at two fundamentally moral issues at stake in cultural representation in educational settings.

First, the question of how cultures are represented in the curriculum is moral in nature because it affects whether certain children are, discursively speaking (i.e., in the official discourses of schooling), absent or present, and whether or not they have voice. This in turn raises the question of who belongs and who does not, and also whether the complexity of a child's heritage and culture (using the word lightly here) is conveyed or not. In chapter two and also above in the section on participation, we argued that whether children get to speak in class, and particularly whether they can initiate dialogue as well as merely respond to it, is a profoundly moral question. Here, we parallel that by suggesting that the question of whether children are represented fully and fairly in the curriculum is also deeply moral in nature. This is particularly so if we consider the connection Bernstein (1990) draws between the how and the what of schooling, that is, the *regulative discourse* and the *instructional discourse* which make up the *pedagogic discourse*, which he acknowledges to be, above all, moral in nature. We argue, then, that the two matters of the participation of non-majority children in teaching and learning and the way they are represented in the curriculum constitute the ways in which cultural representations are played out in the pedagogic discourse. As Dilg (1999) puts it, if our students "do not feel included, if they do not feel part of the focus of their texts or their courses or the process of learning, most of them have neither the power nor the choice to place themselves in a more comfortable or inclusive setting" (p. 9): In other words, if they do not belong in these classes, they do not belong in the broader society, either.

Second, there is a profound moral dilemma in the selection and presentation of curricular materials that represent other cultures. Take *Little House on the Prairie*, for example: Should this book not be used in the classroom, in the hope that, by ignoring the problem (however we choose to define "the problem"), it will go away? Or should the teacher present it as an example of how Indians were often portrayed in the fiction of an earlier age, at the same time risking the possibility that some children will not get the point and will take away only the negative images? And what about representing other countries? It is a practical impossibility to "cover" each country of the world adequately in the course of a year (or even of a whole childhood in school). Yet not to mention countries at all is to render them, and thus their people, invisible. In that respect the authors of the books surveyed above are to be saluted for their attempt to at least mention all the countries of the world, including "obscure" countries such as Belarus or Chad, the location and often even existence of which many adults seem unaware. That they do not succeed in their efforts is not their own failure but, rather, an indication of the impossibility of a truly inclusive multiculturalism. Yet, because it is an impossible struggle, is it one that should be abandoned?

Whatever one's responses to these very difficult questions, one thing remains certain: However cultures are (or are not) represented in curricular materials, it is the teacher who must mediate between those materials and what children take from them. To return to the example of *Little House on the Prairie*, we would not wish to change the book itself. It is what it is — a document from a former time and a particular cultural standpoint. Yet, without changing the text, there are many ways in which teachers can intervene. One is simply to choose alternative readings for the class — this is not book banning, but simply part of the job teachers do. And, as our analysis has shown, this task carries with it considerable moral significance. Another option would be to continue using the book but to do so in order to raise the children's awareness of cultural representation. This in itself could be accomplished by various means: contrasting this text with another, for example, or by incorporating Indian voices into the classroom to express different perspectives.

In any case, the point is that the foundation of the moral dimension of teaching lies not in the material but in the relation between teacher and student. Through the process of mediating potentially dangerous cultural representations, the teacher is in a position to explicate those materials and also to consider the relationship between the cultural representations they contain and the actual children present in the classroom. In effect, she can guide the way the children themselves are represented. And this, in turn—the teacher's moral agency—is a matter of even greater significance than the representations included in the materials. This said, of course, moral uncertainties remain. At each step the teacher faces difficult choices concerning the way children and their cultures are dealt with in the classroom. Yet the morality of these issues inheres not in the inert materials themselves but in the living relations between teacher and students in particular classrooms.

CULTURE, IDENTITY, AND VALUES IN EDUCATION

Culture and Identity

Having looked at the issues of participation and representation, let us now consider the question of *identification*: the emergence of identity in children, especially in minority children. Our central questions are these: Who do you become through your schooling? And what is the moral significance of this process?

The relationship between culture and identity is highly complex. Many scholars in fields such as anthropology and cultural studies have become so wary of the contested notion of *culture*—once the central, defining concept of the field of anthropology—that they have begun to avoid it altogether in their writings. Interestingly, as Atkinson (1999) and others have pointed out, its place has often been taken by *identity*, as if the two terms covered a similar area. Whether or not this is so, the concept of identity lies at the heart of the moral dilemma inherent in the idea of culture. To what extent can a social construction such as culture represent values when, as Maxwell

(1991) points out, morality can be instantiated only by specific individuals? And yet, at the same time, how can an individual have an identity that is in any way meaningful (to him- or herself or to others) without mediating that identity through culture in some way or another? The very notions of individualism and identity are culturally constructed (many languages have no word for "the self," for example). This conundrum, of course, brings in its wake a host of moral questions, many of which we will raise here.

Setting aside for a moment this paradox, it needs to be said that, like the more open-ended, polyvalent, multiple vision of culture outlined above, identity is no longer the fixed, unitary concept it once was. It is, in Norton Peirce's (1995) words, "multiple, a site of struggle, and subject to change" (p. 9). Recent theoretical and empirical research on identity (e.g., Gergen, 1991; Holland et al., 1998; MacClure, 1993; Sarup, 1996) has suggested three basic qualities of identities. First, identities are multiple and in conflict within the individual. Second, identities are not inherent characteristics like our height or the color of our eyes, but rather change over time and according to particular social and cultural contexts. Third, identities are not simply internal, unchanging characteristics; rather, and crucially, they are discursively constructed, maintained, and negotiated.

In education, furthermore, identities are in formation—a process that often is rapid, dramatic, and has untold moral consequences for each child. For this reason, we want to suggest that one crucial aspect of the relationship between culture and morality in education is that of *identification*: the process of both acquiring and applying identities. As this two-part definition implies, there are two sides to this process—that is, to the question posed above of "who children become through their schooling." One is the way in which the children themselves adopt, assume, or claim particular identities for themselves. The second is the way in which identities are assigned to the child by others, especially by those who hold power over the child: teachers, principals, social workers, and so on. This second process—by which the child is identified, labeled, and categorized by those about him or her and, in particular, by those who hold power, such as the teacher and the school administration—is not independent of the first but holds critical importance for it.

Language, Power, and Cultural Identity

In fact, much of what we have said both earlier in this chapter and elsewhere in the book bears directly on the topic of this section. First, it is abundantly clear that, to a significant extent, it is through language and specific forms of discourse that identities are formed, constructed, negotiated, challenged, reinforced, or changed. Foley (1996) gives a penetrating analysis of the way the "silent Indian" is as much a discursive construction as it is a sociocultural reality. Reexamining Philips's (1983) claims about Native-American interactional patterns, Foley suggests that, although Philips's portrayal "has real merit" (p. 81), the "silent Indian" is as much as a "discursively constructed . . . image" (p. 88) as it is an "objective" (p. 87) description of how Indian children behave (see below for more on Foley's analysis).

The labeling of entire ethnic groups is one discursive problem minority children have to face. Another is the danger of being (mis)labeled due to imperfect communications across cultural borders. Grudgeon and Woods (1990) describe how a process of "statementing" set in motion by local authorities led to the categorization of Balbinder, a six-year-old child of Kenyan-Asian parents, as "a child with special needs" (p. 66), against the better judgment of the parents and the researcher, who was "concerned" by the fact that "Balbinder seemed to understand and respond better in Punjabi" (p. 77) than in English, and that this might be a significant part of the problem. The decision taken by the authorities to place Balbinder in special education took him "[o]ut of mainstream education perhaps for the rest of his school career" (p. 83); the process of statementing "disrupted his normal development" (pp. 83–84) and did not take into account "the evident disjuncture between the cultural norms of his home and community and those of the school" (p. 84).

Willett (1995) looks at the case of Xavier, a Spanish-speaking first-grader in a multinational elementary school in the United States. The seating arrangement in the classroom Willett studied—along with behavior norms prevailing among the students regarding, for example, boy–girl relations—made it impossible for Xavier to get the help from peers that he needed to complete his classroom tasks:

> Xavier . . . without alternate sources for help would ask for help from adults more often. Consequently, he began to gain an identity as a needy child who could not work independently. This belief was fed by another belief, explicitly stated by several school personnel, that children from the barrio were semilingual and that their parents were unable to help their children academically. (p. 497)

Willett goes on to describe how Xavier's attempts to resist the imposition of this identity—for example, by refusing to do work from ESL workbooks rather than the phonics books the other children had, and by protesting when he was taken out of class for ESL instruction—"merely confirmed the adults' views about him" (p. 497) as a problematic case. The moral implications of this labeling are considerable: Through an ideologically fed discursive construction of him as a "needy child" from the barrio, Xavier's very identity as a "competent member of the class" (p. 496) was undermined, affecting both the way he was seen by the adults of the school and his entire future as a student—for, as the case of Balbinder mentioned above showed, once such labels are applied, they are notoriously difficult to remove.

Power, too, plays a vital role in the moral construction of identity. It is through hegemonic distributions of power, and through the resistance of the disempowered, that claims and assignations of identity take place. As Harklau (2000) put it, power "can lend a greater sense of authority and sense of reality to some representations [of identity] than others" (p. 40); more specifically, in the case of Harklau's study, "educators' representations of ESOL student identity are more likely to be reflected and reproduced in broader institutional discourses than their students' are" (p. 40). These "discourses" are not merely linguistic categorizations but extend in a Foucaultian sense to "the configuration of programs, placement measures, and evaluation" (p. 63)—all aspects of the educational process that bring with them weighty moral meanings. Furthermore, although many European Americans and other whites do not "see" the workings of power, for most members of minorities they are plain. Indeed, a common definition of racism is the combination of racial prejudice and power. Chang (1996) goes so far as to suggest that it is cultural differences, not gender, that play the most influential role in unequal power relations; McKay and Wong (1996) found that, in the discursive construction of multiple cultural identities in Mandarin-speaking immigrant students in a California middle school, a vital role was played by power relations—specifically, by the children's acceptance of or resistance to their "powerless positioning as 'ESL student'" (p. 592).

Participation and Representation in Identity Formation

It is also, of course, through culturally influenced patterns of participation and representation that identities are shaped. Foley (1996) recounts a telling anecdote from a conversation with Mesquaki clan leader Lee Kingfisher, with whom Foley had attended high school in central Iowa. Foley asked Kingfisher "why he and other Mesquakis were always so quiet in class" (p. 84):

> Lee answered my question with another question, "When you and other whites come out to the settlement, do you talk as much as you do in town?"

I sat there speechless, and Lee sensed he had an anthro-
pologist in his muskrat trap. He said slyly, "Why not?" I had
to answer, "Well, it's a strange situation. Anyone with any
sense would hold back to see how you should act."

That brought a big smile to his face, and Leo [sic] said it
was the same with Mesquakis. He was just trying to say that
Indians are people like everybody else. If you have any
sense, a strange situation calls for less talking. (pp. 84–85)

This simple point uncovers the way in which identity formation takes place through forms of participation and representation. The sheer unfamiliarity of the context—and not
only "cultural differences"—led the Mesquaki students to be
quiet; yet, as Foley goes on to explain, their silence was trans-
formed from a simple behavior to an identifying trait by those
around them in the school—in discursive terms, they became
"silent Indians." Furthermore, the story of the Mesquaki students reveals the complex connections between the identities
assigned to students by teachers and others (such as
researchers) and the identities the students themselves adopt.
Foley reports that in some cases the Mesquaki themselves consciously cooperated in the construction of the "silent Indian"
to serve their own purposes. According to some of his
Mesquaki informants, "Mesquaki kids use the 'silent Indian'
image very effectively to avoid schoolwork" (p. 84). One former student "admitted that they used, as he put it, 'the old
silent Indian thing' to keep white teachers off their backs" (p.
84). The resistance evident in this act shows in a nutshell how
language, power, and culture interrelate in the creation and
negotiation of identity; this process is fundamentally moral
because it affects both who people are, including the values
they hold, and their relations with other people.

The forms of cultural representation found in classroom
materials are also crucial in the development of identity. As
Pagano (1991) points out, in educational settings the processes
of identity formation "involve students locating their own

questions in material to be studied and in identifying with and responding to the questions of others" (p. 257). Because cultural identity is a major part of who one is, the extent to which that cultural identity is present in classroom materials marks the extent to which this significant part of one's identity is visible, acknowledged, and, in moral terms, valued. White children from majority cultures have their identity confirmed and affirmed a thousand times a day in the materials they use; as we saw in the previous section, children from other cultures often do not share this experience.

Such representational experiences, moreover, are not limited to curricular materials. Consider the following anecdote told by one of the high-school students in Dilg's (1999) study, in response to an incident in Sandra Cisneros's *The House on Mango Street* (Cisneros, 1989):

> The teachers have difficulty pronouncing her name or didn't want to try. I can definitely relate to that. One time a woman asked me my name and I told her. She responded, "Well, I can't pronounce that so I'm just going to call you 'girl.'" To me, it was not her inability to say my name, it was her lack of effort to say my name, like it was unimportant, like I was. My name means "beautiful flower, richly endowed." I'm proud of that. I've tried to live up to that name. It really hurt when she didn't note that the name was unique, ask me its meaning, or even try to say it. If you can't take the time to get to know my name, how can you get to know me? (Dilg, 1999, pp. 35–36)

This incident also concerns the formation of identity through representation, and reveals the moral weight this process carries. This student's story goes immediately to the heart of the moral significance of such an apparently simple thing as using (or not using) someone's name. First, to fail to even try to pronounce the name makes it seem "unimportant"—that is, it diminishes its value in the educational setting. Second, for this student, as for anyone else, her name is a crucial part of who she is; the woman's failure to use the name places a huge obstacle in the development of relation between them, and relation, as we have seen, is one of the fundamental building blocks of moral meaning in the classroom.

The Complexity of Cultural Identities

Finally, there is another moral dilemma at the heart of the debates over cultural identity. The process of applying cultural labels cuts both ways. The phrase "silent Indian" (Foley, 1996), for example, marks not just one identity but two—it labels the child both as silent and as Native American. Although, as Foley suggests, the epithet "silent" may be challenged, the underlying category—a racial one—remains. Our question from a moral standpoint is this: Is this indeed the best way to categorize children? That American society (and with it the American educational system) is profoundly racialized is not in question (McCarthy & Crichlow, 1993). But we ask: Are the interests of children of color and of minority cultures best served by being constantly labeled as such? Dilg (1999) rightly points out that, whereas white children have the option of being "color blind," few children of color have this luxury; many of them cannot help but be "highly identified with their race or culture" (p. 50). Yet is it not also true to say that cultural identities represent a reduction, an oversimplification? No doubt this also constitutes a consequence of racializing tendencies in schooling; but, in moral terms, it raises a profound dilemma over the limitations of using racial, cultural, or ethnic categories to define children.

The question of labeling brings with it yet another paradox in the domain of identity. For many minority children and adults, identity is profoundly multiple. There is a long tradition of exploring the dual or multiple sense of identity felt by members of minority groups, by immigrants, and by people of mixed heritage. W. E. B. Du Bois wrote in 1903 of the "twoness" of the black person—"an American, a Negro" (Du Bois, 1903/1989, p. 5). Du Bois described it as "two souls, two thoughts, two unreconciled strivings; two warring ideals in one dark body, whose dogged strength alone keeps it from being torn asunder" (p. 5). This multiplicity has received renewed theoretical attention in recent postmodern and postcolonial accounts of identity, from Bhabha (1994) to Said (1994).

Du Bois added another aspect of this duality: the "double-consciousness" that comes from "always looking at oneself through the eyes of others" (p. 5). This, in turn, has produced the "outgroup preferment" noted in nonwhite children (Davey, 1983, cited in Hatcher & Troyna, 1993). A striking example of this is reported by Tobin (2000). An Asian-American fourth-grader identified the "bad guys" in a movie because of their "Asian eyes," and proceeded to demonstrate by using her fingers to pull back her own eyes (which were already physiologically "Asian") (p. 61). This dislocation of perceived identity indicates the intimate relationship between identities claimed or adopted by children and those created for them by teachers and the media.

Almost a hundred years after Du Bois, Harklau (1999, 2000) studied how the identities of immigrant children are negotiated in high school and subsequently in community college. She notes that, in the community college, immigrant students in ESL classes were repeatedly given assignments on what she calls "'your country' topics" (Harklau, 1999, p. 115): for example, "homeless people in your country," "my country—a great place to visit," or "a holiday of your culture" (Harklau, 2000, p. 55). Such an approach blatantly ignores the complexities of cultural identity in several significant ways. First, it assumes that the student's primary role is as representative of his or her "culture." There is no acknowledgment of the fact that a student may have—indeed, certainly does have—views on his or her "culture" that differ from those of others from the same "culture." Next, as we have repeatedly pointed out, culture is not a monolithic, fixed, unitary thing. Any given culture is in flux, and includes elements that are controversial and about which people take different views (consider American views on the death penalty, for example). Indeed, the very notion of culture is suspect; what we may think of simplistically as, say, Mexican culture or Vietnamese culture is, in fact, a hugely complex and often contradictory amalgam of cultural practices and values from different subgroups of people (classes, ethnicities, regions, professions, institutions, and so on).

Finally, and most importantly from the point of view of identity and identity formation, asking about the student's "own culture" assumes unproblematically and mistakenly that these students "belong" to a single foreign culture. In fact, the students Harklau studied were immigrants to the United States:

> [T]heir lives and cultural identities were situated in the multiethnic, urban US social milieu in which they had grown to adulthood. Their ethnic affiliations were grounded at least as much in a culturally hybrid immigrant community as in their natal countries. Recollections of what the assignments assumed to be their countries were colored by a separation long in time and distance. (Harklau, 2000, p. 55)

Thus, whereas the identity constructed for minority students may be a simplistic and unitary one, the reality is much more complex: The identities that the students' everyday lives require are multiple, hybrid, and shifting (see, for instance, how Harklau's informant Penny uses culturally deictic terms such as "my," "we," and "here" to refer alternately to the United States and Vietnam [p. 56]). This in turn raises yet another moral dilemma for the teacher: How can such multiple identities be acknowledged, supported, and understood in the classroom?

Finally, the matter of how children "from other cultures" (i.e., other than the teacher's own) are represented recalls Noddings's words about "the uniqueness of human encounters" (1984, p. 5). By reducing students to ciphers of their cultures, we are failing to see them as individuals. Noddings's admonition reminds us that children are both representatives of their cultures and individuals in their own right; but it is only by acknowledging the child's individuality that the role of culture can be dealt with. Once again, the complex relationship between culture, identity, and morality creates a moral knot that teachers must untie afresh with each new student.

To conclude, in many ways the process of identity formation is the single most important thing that happens in education, and one that involves all of the aspects of education we have examined in this book: language and discourse, power and authority, and culture. It is a process in which two crucial strands are interwoven: the identities that children adopt, select, or claim for themselves and those assigned to them by others. And it is a process in which the complex realities of cross-cultural encounters make simple, unitary solutions impossible. There is no more important matter than that of who children become through their schooling, whether we mean what kind of people they turn into, what kinds of opportunities become available to them, or any of the many possible other ways of interpreting this question. As we have tried to demonstrate here, there is no matter in the classroom that is more laden with complex and contradictory moral meanings than this very question.

IN LIEU OF A CONCLUSION

In the present chapter as elsewhere in this book, we have raised moral questions rather than seeking to answer them. As elsewhere, our aim is not to adjudicate on these matters, but to point out the ways in which many of the central dilemmas of teachers' daily work can be fully understood only by recognizing their moral substrate.

In this chapter in particular, we want to end by acknowledging that our analysis has only partially uncovered this moral substrate. Many other matters remain unaddressed. For example, we have raised many questions regarding the value-laden nature of the discrepancies that often exist between the culture of the teacher and that of any given student. But we have said little about the equally important discrepancies that can exist between the cultural values of different students in the same classroom. In some contexts the LEP and minority children in a given classroom come from a single cultural background, but in others there are classrooms in which ten or twenty different languages and cultures are represented. The extraordinarily rich nature of what we might call moral contact in such classrooms deserves to be investigated empirically—at present, few such studies have been published.

Another aspect of the interplay between morality and culture in the classroom concerns the teacher's response to alternative cultural values. We have already established that a teacher's actions are profoundly and unavoidably moral in nature, however she acts. We have also seen that the deepest features of culture are evaluative—that is, moral—in nature. Some of these values may be inimical both to the teacher and to the broader society. Then how is the teacher to interact with the children? To challenge the values they bring in to school (about how to dress, how to work, how to speak, how to interact with members of the opposite sex, how to interact with a teacher, and so on) necessarily involves going out on a moral limb. However, it is also true that *not* to present such challenges is tantamount to accepting the status quo. In either case, and whatever the teacher does, her actions will have moral significance. And furthermore, while the ideas presented in this book may be useful for conceptualizing the moral dilemmas teachers face, each new situation and each new moral dynamic will have to be resolved as it occurs: The complexity and sensitivity to context of these matters and the crucial role played by individuals and the relations between them are such that only those individuals can finally take the actions they deem right, based on the unique particulars of the relations in question.

Finally, there is the matter of whether or not there is a universal human morality, with values rising above those encoded in particular cultures. At one level, this is a highly abstract philosophical question. At another level, however, it can be seen as a very practical issue with which teachers struggle every day. For example, we have mentioned the common observation that the majority American culture is predominantly individualistic in character, whereas some cultures represented by minority children have a preference for collaboration and consultation in both educational and other spheres. Yet which of these is "better"? That this is neither a trivial nor a simple question can be seen by the way that educational systems in the United States and elsewhere continue to wrestle with the two options: In contexts from elementary school to college, collaborative activities exist uneasily side by side with individual grading, for example. This ongoing dynamic is a manifestation of the search for universal values. We have not dealt with this question here, but it too forms an important part of the complex moral substrate of teaching and deserves more detailed consideration at both theoretical and empirical levels. The ongoing debate over "cultural relativity" and the value of multiculturalism versus "traditional values" owes much of its rancor to its unwillingness to address this issue head on.

In these and other matters, cultural values can be seen to lie at the heart of many moral dilemmas in the classroom. How can teachers come to see these dilemmas for what they are, and acquire the conceptual and practical tools that will help in resolving them? It is to this matter that we turn next, as we address the consequences of the analysis in the last four chapters for the practice and theory of teacher education and teacher development.

FIVE

Moral Contact, Teacher Education, and Teacher Development

INTRODUCTION

We have argued throughout this book that teaching is fundamentally a moral activity, that classrooms are sites of moral interaction, and that teachers are moral agents. We have done so by examining some of the particular contexts and processes of teaching. Throughout we have acknowledged the high degree of moral complexity and moral ambiguity that teaching entails; teaching is rewarding yet difficult work in which there is little moral certainty. The complexity and uncertainty, however, cannot and must not lead to a moral paralysis that undermines our efforts to educate and care for society's young. Rather, in spite of the complexity and ambiguity, action is called for on the teacher's part, and such action is moral in nature.

What we have offered in the previous chapters is essentially a different view of teaching. It is a view that examines teaching "below the surface" and enables us to see and hear things differently. We are not saying that our view has discovered something new about teaching; teaching has always been a moral enterprise. Rather, we have sought to uncover and make more visible aspects of teaching that, while always central to teaching, are often unseen and unheard. Such a view, we believe, enriches our understanding of teaching, seeing it as both a more complex and a more ambiguous undertaking. In some sense, this view raises the stakes of teaching while adding to its significance.

In this chapter we will consider how our view of teaching as moral action and classrooms as sites of moral interaction might influence the contexts and processes of teacher education and teacher development. We do so by taking the preceding analysis of classrooms and considering its significance for preservice and practicing teachers and for teacher education programs. This chapter is divided into three sections. In the first section, we will consider how a reading of the classroom as a moral context challenges and changes our understandings of the practice of teaching. Here we propose viewing the practice of teaching as one of moral contact among teachers and students. In the second section, we will discuss the implications this different view of teaching has for teacher preparation programs. In the third section, we will explore consequences of our view of classrooms for teacher development and in-service education for practicing teachers.

TEACHING AS MORAL CONTACT

In chapter 1 we outlined our view that teaching is fundamentally relational and that relations, in turn, are fundamentally moral in nature. In subsequent chapters we peeled back the layers of classroom activity to reveal some of the moral meanings hidden there. In doing so, we uncovered the heretofore unseen and unheard moral dimensions of teaching present in the ways language, power, and culture inform teaching and learning. Our examination of these aspects of classroom life has brought us to a different view of teaching. Teaching for us now assumes a greater moral significance and greater complexity and moral ambiguity. In this section, we will outline how a reading of the classroom as a moral context and teachers as moral agents offers a different—and, we believe, more compelling—view of teaching.

Our view embraces teaching as a point of moral contact between teachers and students. We view teachers as moral agents and as the central point of moral contact in the classroom. A point of moral contact is that point, the nexus, where a teacher's personal values and beliefs about teaching, curriculum, and students come into contact with the hopes, dreams, and aspirations of each of the individual students in the classroom. These points of moral contact between teachers and students in classrooms are the quintessence of teaching and learning. They occur when teachers as moral agents plan and design curricula, implement lessons, arrange a variety of classroom activities, and evaluate and assess students and their work. In this view, teaching is an activity involving a deep awareness of the significance of one's choices and how those choices influence the development and well-being of others. An awareness of the moral significance of one's work enlarges the understanding of that work.

A vision of teaching as moral contact between teachers and students during teaching and learning activities requires us to focus our attention on two central qualities of teaching. These qualities are inherent both in the practice of teaching and in conceptions of the moral. The first quality of teaching is that it is a socially negotiated activity. The second is that it involves what we refer to as the *moral sensibilities*. Moral sensibilities are qualities that enable teachers to perceive and act upon the moral dimensions of classroom life.

We want to note here that taking up our view of teaching does not suggest that teachers should become heroes like the teachers portrayed in popular accounts such as *Stand and Deliver* or *Dead Poets Society*. Nor does our view adhere to a particular approach to teaching, such as a social justice orientation (Ayers, Hunt & Quinn, 1998; Beyer, 1996; Goodman, 1992). Although our view is not contradictory or inconsistent with such approaches to teaching, it does not prescribe them.

Rather it entails a commitment to the youth with whom we share our classrooms.

Teaching as a Socially Negotiated Activity

In the preceding chapters we saw that the moral significance of language, power, and culture in the classroom is rooted in the social nature of teaching and learning. Language, power, and culture take on moral dimensions as they involve social contact between and among individuals and groups of individuals. Thus, what makes teaching a moral activity is, to a significant degree, the social negotiation among its participants. The negotiation is realized through the design of curricula, the implementation of lessons, and the exercise of student evaluation and assessment procedures. This means that teaching demands an awareness of the present conditions of students and of oneself as a teacher—that is, that teachers are fully occupied in the present moment with their students, fully with them in discussions and lessons. Noddings refers to such attentiveness as "motivational displacement," by which the concerns and interests of others become our concerns and interests at that moment (1984, 1992), while Hansen calls on teachers to be morally and intellectually attentive to their students (1999).

However, the concerns and interests of the present moment also must be seen against the backdrop of intended, future outcomes or goals. Fully engaging in a teaching encounter necessitates being able to place the present moment in the context of past experiences and future hopes. As Hansen notes, "teaching is an act that, when done well, fully occupies the present moment, but also always with an eye on the future" (1995, p. 161). Although some of our most memorable teaching moments can be described as occurring "when time seemed to be suspended," those times may have been possible only when our knowledge from past experiences prepared us to be open to present possibilities in light of what we hoped for our students. The convergence of past understandings and knowledge with present awareness of the student's conditions and the teacher's vision underscores our earlier discussion of the importance of context in a moral reading of teaching.

That teaching is a socially negotiated activity also means that it is a highly contextualized activity. Indeed, in each of the preceding chapters we illustrated how teachers and students were deeply involved in negotiations about the meanings of events, actions, and words. Our main point, and one that we emphasized in the examples, is that the moral is to be found both in the very act of negotiation and in the meanings that are negotiated. Such teaching defies a linear and formulaic approach. It is only in realizing and acknowledging this moral significance that teaching as a socially negotiated practice becomes a point of moral contact. As such, teaching as a socially negotiated activity requires the cultivation of moral sensibilities.

Teaching as Cultivating Moral Sensibilities

To engage in teaching as moral contact requires the sensitivity to see and hear the moral that is constantly present in classroom life and activities. It requires the initiative and the ability to take actions we may find initially uncomfortable. In the absence of these sensitivities, abilities, and initiatives, we risk a practice of teaching that misses the moral at best, or at worst becomes a cookbook, technocratic activity. Teachers become sensitive to the moral by cultivating, with the help of others and through their own efforts, a set of moral sensibilities. The sensibilities include moral perception for perceiving the moral in their classroom practices and curricula; moral imagination for seeing what it is that schools, classrooms, and students can become; moral reflection to critically examine how the policies, procedures, and practices of schools and classrooms create moral meanings for teachers and students; and moral courage to engage in all of the above and to take action accordingly.

Moral sensibilities in their totality may function as a sort of moral theory, the basis of a guide for moral action. Indeed, a view of teaching as moral contact necessitates just such a way of examining and reflecting upon one's actions as a teacher. Dewey notes that moral theory "emerges when men [sic] are confronted with situations in which different desires promise opposed goods and in which incompatible courses of action seem to be morally justified" (Dewey & Tufts, 1936, p. 137). Cultivating moral sensibilities provides just that—a moral theory to guide the actions of teachers.

Our view differs from one that focuses on how virtues are made visible in teaching and enacted by teachers as the manner of teaching (Fenstermacher, 1992, 1999). This line of research seeks to illustrate how such virtues as bravery, truthfulness, wit, mildness, magnanimity, magnificence, generosity, temperance, and justice are evidenced in teachers' conduct in the classroom (Fallona, 2000). We acknowledge the central importance of these virtues for conceptualizing teaching as a moral activity. Teaching as moral contact presupposes the existence and enactment of these virtues in teachers' practice, and in part they form a core of the moral dimensions of teaching. But it is the cultivation of moral sensibilities that makes the recognition of these virtues in teaching possible while at the same time advancing a means for nurturing them.

Moral Perception

The perceptions teachers have of themselves, their students, and the practice of teaching guide their work and the choices they make about how and what to teach. Planning curricula and activities that engage and challenge students at the edges of their knowledge and understandings; knowing how to respond to students with the right combination of directness, firmness, and caring when they misbehave; being attentive to the many subtle and sometimes not so subtle messages which indicate that a student is angry, discouraged, alienated, inspired, or feeling any one of a number of different emotions—all of these require a highly tuned sense of perception. To undertake the myriad daily activities of teaching requires the ability to recognize and respond meaningfully, effectively, and thoughtfully to the needs and interests of our students.

Moral perception attunes teachers' sensitivities to the particular needs and concerns of each student in their classroom, and enables teachers to recognize and respond to these needs and concerns. This process "involves sympathetic connection of the kind that comes only through intimate involvement in the everyday drama of the classroom" (Simpson & Garrison, 1995, p. 252). Such a sympathetic connection to students involves emotion, patience, and imagination. Moral perception also entails the ability to perceive the moral in teaching that can create, in effect, a moral context in the classroom.

Imagine meeting your class, whether it is a group of kindergartners or ninth graders at the beginning of the year, or a class of college juniors at the start of a new semester. Each of us may feel to varying degrees excitement, anxiety, apprehension, joy, fear—the list could go on. Our emotions can alter our beliefs about others and the situations in which we find ourselves. Our emotions influence what we perceive about ourselves and others and the meanings we give to those perceptions. Is that a grin or a smirk on the face of the student in the front row? Does it indicate an eagerness to get started with the curriculum and activities you have planned or a readiness to give you fits from the get-go? Is that nervous talking between those two in the back row, or are they going to chat it up all the time? And over on the side of the room, are those downward glances a bit of shyness or feelings of inadequacy before school has even started?

As individuals, we vary not only in the degree to which we are sensitive to certain particular features of a situation, but also in the range of situational and contextual features that we perceive. Blum notes that moral perception is often seen as "one single kind of moral/psychological process" or as a "unitary faculty." This is problematic, for it does not account for the myriad complex ways in which individuals may have "multifarious sensitivities" (1994, p. 47). In other words, some individuals may have finely honed moral sensitivities in perceiving the distinct features of situations involving, say, racism and sexism, whereas others may be more highly tuned to perceiving injustices resulting from a lack of sensitivity to the feelings of children. We all may have particular moral sensitivities and particular moral blind spots. And the blind spots can influence what it is we perceive and ultimately how we respond to individuals and situations. The fact that we all have blind spots in our ability to perceive the moral in situations speaks to the importance of continually cultivating moral perception in both new and experienced teachers. We will address this in more detail in the section on recommendations for teacher education programs.

Without moral perception we have a limited view of our students; a smaller vision of our work as teachers; a limited ability to respond to students in attentive, thoughtful, and effective ways; and a lessened image of what our students and we ourselves can become. Moral perception, then, is about being attuned to what we see, sense, feel, and imagine. Here we see a connection between moral perception and moral imagination.

Moral Imagination

Moral imagination means having a vision of the classrooms, the society, and the world we want to create through our work as teachers and teacher educators (Coles, 1989). It means having a vision of who students can become as individuals, as learners, and as members of society. We use moral imagination, according to Green, when we speak to others about the chasm that exists between "society as it is . . . and society as it would be if it were all that its members think it ought to be" (1999, p. 111). As such, moral imagination is rooted in hope as it looks to the future. Hope is not merely wishful thinking;

it is bound to reality because we hope for what we know is in the realm of possibility. It is by having an understanding of the collected traditions of the practice of teaching that we can imagine what could or should be. Thus, for teachers and teacher educators a moral imagination requires a connection to the collected traditions of the past, while at the same time remaining cognizant of the realities of present conditions.

The gulf between competing visions of what is and what could be underscores the importance of teachers and teacher educators having a clear understanding of what the current practices and conditions of schooling are like for themselves and for their students—and this involves critique. Moral imagination as critique involves a critical examination of present circumstances, situations, teaching practices, and so on in light of a vision of what could or should be. Put differently, moral imagination as critique is not just about critiquing the present; rather, we are challenged to propose a vision for the future. This critique, then, moves beyond the many negative portrayals of the current conditions of schooling, the all-too-frequent school and teacher bashing evident in much of the popular press. Through this critique we can envision new possibilities that encompass changes in practice as well as our understandings of concepts and constructs central to our work as teachers. For example, childhood as a period or stage of life is sometimes portrayed as lacking value in and of itself because children are seen as always becoming, yet never arriving into personhood until they become adults. Childhood is taken for granted as something we pass through on our way to a more meaningful period—adulthood (Canella, 1997). A critique of this view of childhood demands that we vest present experiences with importance and significance, as they contribute to our knowledge of each person as a unique individual, yet also provide a glimpse of what that individual might become.

Moral Reflection

Reflection has been much talked about in education and teacher education. The use of reflection in teaching, especially as a means of understanding ways of guiding and improving practice, appears under a variety of terms, including reflective practice, reflexive teaching, and personal practical knowledge. The focus of these practices is to bring past experiences and our recollections and evaluations of them to bear on our current teaching practices as well as in plans for changing and improving future practices. Yet the deep meaning of reflection—moral reflection, considered here—has to do with what Green (1984, 1999) refers to as *conscience*. For Green, conscience means "reflexive judgment about things that matter" (1999, p. 21). The notion of conscience as reflexive judgment fits our discussion of moral reflection because it is, in Green's words, "judgment that each of us makes in our own case" (p. 21). Green makes two important points about conscience that are directly applicable to moral reflection. First, conscience has an imminent quality to it in that the judgments are self-given. Within this claim, however, there is a second important feature: Judgments of conscience have authority to them. This authoritative voice, though, is in the form of a "distant, impartial, disinterested perspective" and, thus, conscience "must be understood as both imminent and distant, both self-given and authoritative" (p. 22).

Green's second point broadens the areas of activity upon which conscience comments. He believes that conscience "is capable of commenting upon matters that lie far beyond the boundaries of morality narrowly conceived" (1999, p. 22). They are judgments upon things that can be done well or badly. Such a view can "incorporate self-judgment not only in relation to moral conduct . . . but also to personal ideals, social memberships, and standards of craft, including even the exercise of intellectual skills" (p. 22). Green's view resonates with Jackson et al.'s (1993) notion of worthwhileness, in that doing things well imbues them with worth; they become things that matter—and they matter in a moral way. What makes reflection moral, then, and why reflection is important from a moral perspective is that it is an act of conscience. Such reflection provides the grounding needed to address the moral complexity and ambiguity that is inherent in teaching.

Moral Courage

Courage, according to Sockett, "is a virtue that describes how a person, often selflessly, behaves in difficult and adverse circumstances that demand the use of practical reason and judgment in pursuit of long-term commitments that are morally desirable" (1993, p. 74). There are obviously heroic examples of courage; indeed, we may quickly associate courage with heroism. Sockett (1993) presents examples of exemplary courageous teachers, such as Jaime Escalante, as depicted in *Stand and Deliver*, and John Keating from *Dead Poets Society*.

We believe, however, that it is equally important to have a more prosaic definition of courage. From this perspective, to act with courage is to act upon that for which one has great passion, whether it be for another individual (such as a friend or one's students) or for an idea, ideal, or practice. This is the courage that can be called strength in times of adversity. But here too adversity has a prosaic meaning. What does this kind of prosaic courage look like? One example familiar to teachers and parents is the courage and strength summoned to "go on." For parents it is often visible as answering, again and again, the same series of "why" questions so much a part of two-year-olds' vocabulary and way of thinking. It takes courage—and, yes, strength—to submit oneself to endless inquiry about "why, why, why . . ." The same is true for teachers. For teachers, courage appears as the willingness to engage, again and again, day after day, with students in a teaching situation until they "get it," until we and they express an understanding of or grasp the concept, thought, idea, or skill. Such courage exists, at times, when there is little if any certainty that what we are doing has a long-term effect. For Fallona (2000), whose research is based on an Aristotelian framework, the virtue of bravery would encompass the qualities we consider here. Yet bravery, the "making of judgments in troubled circumstances about what is to be done and how to accomplish it" (p. 686), seems again to be beyond our focus on a more prosaic view of

courage. Rather, we see the courage of constancy, the courage
and strength to continually be there for the persons we are
teaching, to exemplify our notion of moral courage as it is
played out in the day-to-day life of the classroom.

Beyer (1996) and Ayers and Ford (1996) offer a series of por-
traits of teachers who exemplify this notion of "courage of
constancy" as they engage in teaching for social justice. For
these individuals, courage takes the form of working within
the system to establish democratic classrooms. In some
schools and systems this is a tremendously difficult task, but
they teach out of their passion for their students, their practice, and their subject. Similarly, Beane (1997) offers examples
of teachers willing to engage in the difficult work of curriculum integration in the face of criticism and skepticism from
colleagues, administrators, and parents. Beane says that these
teachers "are not superwomen or supermen. They are real
teachers leading real lives and working in real schools with
real young people" (p. 70). All of these examples show teachers living out the quality of moral courage.

Moral Action: Addressing Moral Complexity and Moral Ambiguity

Cultivating moral sensibilities prepares us for facing the
tremendous moral complexity and moral ambiguity that is part
of teaching in all types of classrooms. Moral ambiguity and
moral complexity arise when a middle-school student uses a
racial slur in reference to a classmate; when, with the teacher
and class waiting and looking on, a third-grader dissolves into
tears as an attempt to answer a question grows longer and more
troubled, revealing to all a lack of competence; when a high-
school student questioning whether the Holocaust actually
occurred decides that, if it did happen, it may have been justified; when, at any level of schooling, teaching for the test takes
precedence over in-depth study of a topic; and in countless
other situations. While most (hopefully all) would see the need

to deal with a racial slur as unambiguous, how an individual teacher addresses that situation can be tremendously complex, with no small part of the complexity having to do with how the teacher will treat the students involved. Other situations outlined above are equally of moral import and place teachers in ambiguous and complex situations.

The world of the classroom in many ways resembles the postmodern world as described by Bauman (1993, 1995, 1997), Lather (1991, 1992), and others. According to Bauman, postmodernity moves us away from the notions of a single Truth, often framed as a metanarrative, toward an understanding of the importance of meaning making; from the belief in and reliance upon a singular view of the world and of practices that can be identified toward the recognition of multiple perspectives that are drawn upon as guides for action and practices; from the security and feeling of certainty in our causes and practices toward the liberating yet at times terrifying epiphany of the ambiguous nature of the world. It is not that casting a moral lens on classrooms means adopting a postmodern view of teaching practices. But in seeking to uncover and examine the moral in teaching practices, we become much more aware of the ambiguities and complexities of classroom life.

How can the cultivation of these moral sensibilities better prepare teachers for the morally complex and morally ambiguous world of the classroom? How can the enhancement of these abilities heighten teachers' sensitivity to the moral dimensions of teaching? That is, how can they help teachers perceive the often subtle moral dimensions of classroom life? Similarly, how can they enrich teachers' practice by guiding teaching in ways that serve rather than obscure the moral dignity of students and teachers alike?

We offer the following answers, based on the description of each of the moral sensibilities outlined above. First, moral sensibilities can point out to us the normative dimensions of teaching practices. This is important, because the normative

aspects of teaching practices often either operate below conscious awareness or, if present in our awareness, are taken for
granted and remain unquestioned (that is, free from the
scrutiny of moral reflection). Through moral perception, moral
imagination, and moral reflection, it is possible to discern and
clarify principles that can serve as guides for practice. This is
not an attempt to prescribe practice; rather, the hope is that
moral sensibilities will be brought to a sustained examination
of our goals and the practices used to reach those goals.

Second, the moral sensibilities help us drink in the information necessary for moral judgment. They draw our attention to the moral dimensions of classroom life by attuning us
to the subtle and highly nuanced ways in which the moral is
present in teaching practices and curricula. On the other
hand, they can lead us to question taken-for-granted practices.
Each of these instances provides us with important information and insights that contribute to our ability to make moral
judgments. By moral judgment, we partially mean "the faculty of insight into how general rules are to be applied in particular situations" (Larmore, 1987, p. ix).

This leads to a third point. Larmore (1987, p. ix) goes on to
say: "Rules are undeniably a necessary feature of morality, but
morality does not consist merely in the conscientious adher-
ence to rules." Indeed, moral sensibilities focus our attention
on those *particular* aspects of an individual, a behavior, an
activity, or a context that bring the moral to the foreground
and are essential components in the determination of our
actions. Blum (1994) says that, not only are the particularities
of a situation important in making moral judgments, but individuals can and do vary greatly in their abilities to perceive
particular aspects of an individual, situation, or context.

Our message is that teachers *do* have a moral sense. Teachers inherently know that teaching is a moral activity. What
we are suggesting are ways of confirming, affirming, and nurturing that awareness. Likewise, we feel it is essential that
teacher educators make the cultivation of moral sensibilities a

central goal of teacher education programs. To that end, we believe it is crucial that courses and field experiences focusing on the development of subject matter and pedagogical expertise be organized in such a way that the content and experiences are viewed through a moral lens. One place to begin is to acknowledge the beliefs and values that preservice students bring with them into teacher education programs. Would-be teachers come to our teacher education programs with their own views and notions about teaching and about the teachers they hope to become. They have shaped their views through their own experiences in schools. Some may want to emulate teachers who have encouraged and inspired them; others may want to be teachers as a form of resistance, to change teaching practices they experienced and felt were intolerable. A central role of teacher education programs, then, should be to help students develop the moral sensibilities so that they see their views and notions about teaching as a moral vision of teaching.

A MORAL PERSPECTIVE ON TEACHER EDUCATION

In this section, we examine the implications of our view of the practice of teaching for teacher education. We will address the following questions: How can teacher education programs prepare preservice teachers with the dispositions and abilities to see and hear the moral in teaching practices and curricula? How can preservice teachers develop and refine moral reflection? In addressing these questions, we will make a number of proposals.

Viewing teaching as a moral activity means that teacher education is also inherently a moral activity. Approaching teacher education as a moral activity can ensure that the courses, field experiences, and other activities in which preservice teachers engage are developing the abilities, dispositions, and skills to see and hear the moral in teaching. What we describe below are features of a quality teacher education program that support and nurture the development of moral sensibilities. We see them as critical yet not as defining features of any program. In other words, we are not advocating a particular type of teacher education program, such as one whose primary focus is social justice (Ayers & Ford, 1996; Beyer, 1996) or one based on constructivist theory (Richardson, 1997), both of which can serve as guiding frameworks. Rather, because we believe that developing moral sensibilities in preservice teachers provides a basis for envisioning and enacting teaching as a moral activity, and that continued attention to them enhances the practice of experienced teachers, we advocate that they be a central feature of any teacher education and professional development program.

In what follows, we examine a number of features of teacher education and professional development programs. By examining these aspects of teacher education, we can address the questions set forth at the beginning of this section. The features of teacher education and professional development programs that we examine are those that are fairly common and widely implemented. We are not advocating new reforms for teacher education and professional development. Numerous authors have addressed this topic (e.g., Darling-Hammond, Wise, & Klein, 1995; Goodlad, 1990, 1994; Koppich, 2000; Zeichner, 2000; Zeichner, Malnick, & Gomez, 1996). Our intent here is not to review this literature. Rather, our goal is to bring to the fore the moral dimensions of teaching. For our purposes here, this means explicating how features and experiences common to different kinds of teacher education programs can develop and nurture the moral sensibilities outlined above. We will consider the features and experiences of preservice programs, which include redefining the teacher–student relationship, examining the personal beliefs and philosophies of students entering preservice programs, recontextualizing methods courses and content knowledge, and ensuring authentic field experiences and student teaching activities.

Redefining the Teacher–Student Relationship

Fundamental to conceptualizing the moral nature of teaching and learning activities undertaken in preschool through graduate-level classrooms is an understanding of the relationships that are engendered between teachers and students and among students. Therefore, the first implication of a focus on nurturing moral sensibilities in preservice students involves redefining the relationships between teachers and students and among students in teacher education programs.

Redefining the teacher–student relationship means positioning ourselves differently in relation to our students and to the content we teach (Harre & Langenhove, 1999). This means rethinking how power and authority shape our relationships with students. For some, the result is to share power and authority with students in the classroom (Ellsworth, 1989, 1997; Manke, 1997; Oyler, 1996). For others, it may mean becoming co-learners and inquirers with students. Of course, sharing power and authority can take other forms. Regardless of the form such changes take, they can have a profound influence on teaching practices.

There is an old adage that says, "we tend to teach the way we were taught." There seems to be a fair amount of truth in this saying, as borne out by research (e.g. Lortie, 1975) as well as by much anecdotal evidence. What this means is that, unless concerted and explicit efforts are made to change preservice students' experiences with their teachers in their own classes, the practices we most hope to instill in our students may not take root, and the practices we most hope to change may persist.

To address this, and at the risk of sounding trite, we can refer to another old adage that says we should teach our students as we would have them teach their students. The question before us is this: How can we nurture moral sensibilities in our preservice students when we engage them in the types of teaching practices we hope they will implement with their students? Although certainly not a new thought to teacher education, a redefinition of the teacher–student relationship through a practice of teaching our preservice students as we would have them teach their students is important for at least two reasons.

The first reason has to do with making visible and explicit key features of the teacher–student relationship as our relationships unfold in class with students. During the time we spend with students in a course, we can engage them in conversation about the nature of the relationships we want to nurture, why it is important to us, and how various activities will contribute to their development. By making explicit the features that are central to positive, productive, and moral teacher–student relationships, we engage students in a discussion of moral sensibilities while simultaneously modeling. An examination of teacher–student relationships is part moral reflection, part moral courage, and part moral imagination. It is moral reflection because it entails the careful observation of, thinking about, and critique of how we are building relationships with our students. The close scrutiny of our actions and thoughts is never easy. Even when undertaken in private—that is, when we keep our reflections to ourselves—it requires courage, because we are faced with our shortcomings and failings. When our reflections occur in the public realm of the classroom, a greater degree of courage is summoned because we are now vulnerable to the critique of others as well as ourselves. Thus each case of reflection, whether private or public, is a moral venture, meaning it requires moral courage. Finally, it is part moral imagination because the critique of our practices inherent in moral reflection becomes possible only when we imagine what could be. The image of a different type of classroom, one in which different relationships with and among students occur, is created and rises up from our moral imagination. By making visible the features of teacher–student relationships that we value and the means through which we hope to nurture those features, we invite students into an apprenticeship (Lave & Chailkin, 1993) in the moral sensibilities: moral reflection, moral courage, and moral imagination.

A second reason for teaching students as we would have them teach their students is that we can assist students in critically reflecting on their own immediate and past experiences in classrooms as students. In the previous paragraph, engagement in moral reflection and in the development of moral sensibilities occurred from the teacher's perspective. This is important because our students *will be* teachers and therefore need to learn how to arrange classrooms, plan and teach lessons, and nurture positive relations among the children in their room, all the time remaining cognizant of the moral meanings these activities have for students. When we engage our students in an examination of their own experiences as students in present as well as past classes, we reverse the vantage point from which they view moral sensibilities. Recollections of feeling discouraged, disappointed, bored, alienated, or ignored can be poignant examples of what schooling might be like in the absence of moral sensibilities. Conversely, recalling situations when they felt supported, encouraged, challenged, or excited about learning can enable students to understand how the possible enactment of moral sensibilities by their teachers may have accounted for the positive experiences they met.

Redefining the teacher–student relationship by sharing power and authority with students, becoming co-learners and inquirers with our students, or engaging in other changes in classroom and teaching practices is to some extent dependent upon our willingness to critically examine our own teaching practices, our own theories of teaching and learning, and the content which we teach and which our students will teach. By making our critical examination explicit to our students, they can gain insights into what moral imagination, moral courage, and moral reflection are, what they "look like," and how they function in the real world of classrooms. In doing so, we can make explicit how we have forged a philosophy of teaching and an educational theory from our practical experiences as teachers (Whitehead, 1993). Finally, explicit critical moral reflection can nurture in students the moral sensibilities necessary to see themselves as teachers and moral agents in the lives of their own students.

Examining Personal Beliefs and Philosophies

Preservice teachers enter teacher education programs with implicit theories and philosophies of teaching. Yet their implicit views are often ignored and left unexamined. As teacher educators, we implore preservice teachers to recognize and affirm the knowledge, beliefs, values, and skills that children bring with them to the classroom; yet we often fail to acknowledge the beliefs, knowledge, values, and skills preservice teachers bring with them to teacher education programs. As teacher educators, we are sometimes too quick to begin socializing students into ways of thinking about teaching and learning. The failure to recognize students' own implicit beliefs, most of which they have developed during their many years in classrooms as students, may leave students feeling that their beliefs and personal philosophies are of little value, and this is a moral judgment. What often results is that, rather than engaging students in an examination of their own personal beliefs and philosophies in light of their current experiences in their teacher education program, students' beliefs and personal philosophies end up being papered over by the imposition of the values and philosophies espoused by the teacher educator and the teacher education program.

It is crucial to students' development as teachers that they engage continuously throughout their teacher education program in opportunities to examine, test, and reformulate their beliefs and personal philosophies. Such experiences allow for changes in students' taken-for-granted views (Bowers, 1984, 1995; McCadden, 1998) and are the heart of moral reflection.

Recontextualizing Methods and Subject Matter Courses

An appreciation of the moral in teaching and of the self as a moral agent in the lives of students necessitates a shift in the purpose, focus, and content of methods and subject matter courses. By methods courses we mean courses whose purpose and content are to provide students with the knowledge and skills to prepare, implement, and assess lessons and activities that will be taught in a variety of disciplines (e.g., math, science, and social studies). On the other hand, in subject matter courses preservice teachers learn the content of the different disciplines that they, in turn, will teach their students. Because the courses have different purposes, the ways in which they are infused with an understanding of the moral underpinnings of their content also differs. With regard to methods courses, this means that how one teaches, the "method" used, must be understood in the broader context of how employing a particular method to teach a specific content to a group of students will influence the growth and development of those individuals. In other words, how and what one teaches *is* of moral import. Yet, seldom, it seems, is this point included in discussions in methods courses. Rather, consideration more often is given to the influence of a particular method on the development of critical thinking skills, writing abilities, or any number of other aspects of learning. It is not that these are secondary to moral considerations. Indeed, the acquisition of such knowledge and skills is what parents expect when they send their children to school and what school systems have outlined in their goals and objectives for their students. Yet our point throughout has been that these aspects of teaching cannot be seen in separation from their moral significance.

Likewise, a number of concerns arise concerning the content of subject matter courses. To some extent these were addressed in chapter 4 with regard to the ways nonmajority people and cultures are represented in textbooks. As we noted, problems with representation fall into two categories: acts of omission and acts of commission. We pointed out that a number of minority students find themselves absent not only from course textbooks but more generally from course syllabi. Put differently, even if they are omitted from the textbook, seldom is that omission addressed by class discussion or the presentation of other source materials. Ultimately, omission from the textbook results in omission from the course. On the other hand, in those instances when the textbook does provide some coverage of different minority and ethnic groups, what is presented often suffers from misinformation, bias, and even racism. As we noted, such representations raise concerns about the truthfulness of the information presented and how it contributes to the identities students construct for themselves and others. Similarly, then, our concerns focus on the truthfulness of the content students encounter in any and all of their courses that are part of their teacher education program. Numerous calls have been made for teaching candidates to be well versed in their subject areas (e.g., Goodlad, 1990, 1994; Zeichner, Melnick, & Gomez, 1996). These calls have reflected the general public's concern that teachers "can't teach what they don't know." Yet, while it is important that teachers "know their stuff," it is equally important that as part of the process of acquiring that knowledge they also acquire the dispositions and skills—some might say the connoisseurship and reflection—necessary to critically evaluate the knowledge claims put before them. Subject matter courses are as much about educating students about how to be educated persons as they are about acquiring knowledge. To pursue the latter without accomplishing the former falls short of nurturing in students the sensibility of moral reflection.

One implication of these views is that teacher education is part of the overall purpose of those institutions of higher education that prepare students for careers in teaching. Teacher education occurs in every class and activity in which teaching candidates participate. In other words, teacher education extends within institutions far beyond the schools and colleges of education and departments of curriculum and instruction traditionally seen as responsible for teacher preparation. That teacher education becomes the broader responsibility of universities and colleges means that partnerships should be forged between and among the various groups and departments presently offering courses and other educational experiences to students in preservice teacher education programs.

Field Experiences and Student Teaching

Field experiences (or *practica*, as they are sometimes called) are often attached to or integrated into methods courses. Their purpose is to provide opportunities for preservice students to observe and teach in actual classroom settings. The goal is for students to relate what they have read, discussed, and learned in campus-based courses to real children in actual classrooms. This often involves students making careful observations of the teacher and students in the class along with the preparation, teaching, and evaluation of their own lesson plans. Such experiences are a constant feature of teacher education programs. Student teaching, on the other hand, is most often a total immersion into the classroom of a supervising or mentor teacher. Student teachers are in the classroom all day, every day for an entire term or semester. The student-teaching experience is often accompanied by a seminar led by a faculty member. Taken together, student teaching and the seminar provide the capstone experience of many teacher education programs.

Students often report how busy they are during their field practica and student teaching experiences. Amid this busyness, unless students are drawn to reflect upon their experiences, they are apt to miss out on important aspects of their teaching. Often these are the moral dimensions of their practices. Because they provide links between teacher education courses and the practice of teaching in the real world, field experiences and student teaching should provide ideal opportunities to nurture moral sensibilities. Yet, if these experiences focus primarily or solely on the technical and pragmatic aspects of teaching, the opportunity for students to develop moral sensibilities can be lost. As students enter classrooms, whether during field experiences or student teaching, they become moral agents in the lives of the children in those classrooms. Developing an understanding of this role goes hand in hand with the development of moral sensibilities. For this reason, university supervisors and classroom teachers play a key role in supporting students' acquisition of moral sensibilities during field experiences and student teaching.

A central role for university supervisors is to bring to students' awareness, through the moral sensibilities, just how as moral agents they exert an influence on the children and youth in their care. By directing their students' attention to particular aspects of classroom activities and teaching practices, university supervisors can nurture moral reflection, moral perception, and moral imagination in their students. For example, developing an understanding of the inner workings of schooling in general, and of the school that is the site of the field practicum or student-teaching experience in particular, is an important part of becoming an effective and morally aware teacher. Because of the demands of student teaching and all its accompanying anxiety, the excitement of finally getting to teach, the drive to be a good student teacher and to please the cooperating teacher, it can be easy for students to focus only on the immediate tasks of planning and implementing their lessons and to lose sight of one part of the big picture—namely, the moral part of their work. In other words, students can get so caught up in the requirements of student teaching that, unless someone calls them to look closely at what they are doing, they may find themselves participating in practices without critical moral reflection.

In the previous chapters we delineated some of the moral dimensions of teaching practices as they pertain to language, power and authority, and culture. Here we briefly revisit those topics, focusing on how questions raised in those chapters can serve to nurture the moral sensibilities of preservice students. Through careful observation, discussion, and questioning, supervisors can reflect with their students on the moral dimensions of the schools and classrooms in which they are placed and of the teaching practices of which they are a part. Are the practices in which they find themselves as teachers those practices that we, as their teachers, hoped they would implement and that they as teachers now want to implement? Do they speak to their students during lessons and activities in ways that engage and challenge them as active learners? Are there opportunities for all students to participate in lessons in ways that are meaningful to them? Are language practices inclusive of all students and their abilities, or do they marginalize or exclude language minority students? How do they exercise their authority as teachers? How is this manifested in the ways they teach and evaluate their students? How are they creating a classroom environment in which students can represent themselves and find themselves represented in ways that are authentic and respectful of their personhood and culture? Are they developing an awareness of the moral significance and moral meanings of the policies, practices, routines, and rituals of the classroom and the school in which they are placed? How does a moral perspective challenge their taken-for-granted views? Such reflection hones student teachers' moral perception and their ability to look deeply for the moral influence and moral meanings that their actions as teachers have on their students.

Engaging in this type of moral reflection and moral perception brings students face to face with the difficult realities of being a reflective practitioner. Asking questions that call students to reflect upon practice can lead to unsettling answers, which in turn may lead students to develop another practice: the continual critical examination of their teaching philosophies and practices. However, we also must be cognizant of the implications that reflection has for teaching practices.

Changes in teaching practices may call for moral courage to resist implementing practices that students feel maintain and support current inequities in school, such as de facto tracking of students (Brantlinger, 1993). A cautionary note is important here: Such resistance can jeopardize student teachers' evaluations, perhaps leaving them in the position of having to choose between their own welfare and that of their students. But of its very nature, this, too, calls for moral reflection on the part of the student teacher and supervisor.

Summary

Engaging students in conversation and asking them questions about their experiences in classrooms can raise their awareness of the moral implications of their work as teachers. Such interactions with university supervisors and classroom teachers are ways for students to develop and hone their capacity to perceive the moral. But all of this rests upon the assumption that we as teacher educators have taken the time and put in the difficult work to develop our own moral sensibilities. Calling on our students to reflect upon the moral meanings of what they perceive and do in classrooms and our suggestions for actions, moral and otherwise, are possible and moral in their own right, to the extent that we are morally attuned to our own practices as teacher educators. If we have attuned our own moral sensibilities to perceiving the moral in classrooms, we can draw our students' attention to pertinent situations, actions, practices, and policies of classrooms and to the moral meanings they may have for themselves as teachers and for their students. Some of these may be fairly obvious (such as tracking), others may be much more subtle but no less morally meaningful. The point here is that we cannot give our students what we do not have. In order to nurture in others those moral sensibilities we believe central to the moral practice of teaching, we must be committed to nurturing the same moral sensibilities within ourselves.

MORALITY AND TEACHER DEVELOPMENT

In this section we consider the implications that a reading of the classroom as a moral context has for professional development. Here we ask, what does accepting our view of the moral aspects of teaching mean for the professional development of teachers? A final point needs to be made here. Our intent is not to review the literature on teacher development but rather, as noted above, to outline the implications our perspective has for professional development practices.

Teacher Development as a Moral Activity

We believe a moral reading of classroom events can affect teachers' professional development, because it can lead to an awareness of the moral meanings of their actions as teachers and thus can lead to changes both in understandings of teaching and in teaching practices and curriculum development. We follow Whitehead's (1993) suggestion that the fundamental question for all teachers regarding their professional development should be this: How do I improve my practice? As a corollary to this question, Whitehead poses a second question to teachers that focuses on those who are taught, namely: How do I improve my students' learning? In asking these two questions Whitehead seeks to understand how "the professional development of teachers is related to improving the quality of pupils' learning" (1993, p. 27). Whitehead's view of professional development as improving teaching practices with the intent of improving students' learning, and thus contributing to their betterment as individuals, is professional development as a moral activity, since it focuses on the teacher–student relation. However, there is another way in which professional development as envisioned and practiced by Whitehead and his students is a profoundly and inherently moral activity.

In Whitehead's view, professional development as improving one's teaching practice involves appealing to teachers' "experience of existing as a living contradiction" by asking, "How do I live my values more fully in my practice?" (1993, p. 17). For Whitehead, a living contradiction involves "holding educational values whilst at the same time negating them" in one's teaching practices (p. 71). In other words, at the core of Whitehead's view of professional development as improving practice is a form of inquiry, a type of action research, that asks teachers to examine how and why the values, beliefs, and theories they hold about teaching are contradicted by their teaching practices. Professional development, then, is a moral activity because it involves a clash between values and beliefs on the one hand and teaching practices on the other.

Professional development as a means of facing up to one's living contradictions is a matter of values and integrity. As teachers face up to an examination of the contradictions between their beliefs and their teaching practices, they become the source of their own professional development. Teachers' inquiry into their own teaching practices becomes the impetus for change. We believe this type of change, which occurs in the way individual teachers think—in one's own head, so to speak—is the most lasting and significant (Whitehead, 1993). As Bell and Gilbert note: "Teacher development can be viewed as teachers learning, rather than as others getting teachers to change" (1996, p. 33). Thus, the change that occurs is driven from teachers' own inquiry about their own practice rather than coming from sources, be they individuals or theories, that exist outside of their practice.

Whitehead's views on professional development fit nicely with our view of teacher professional development as an inherently moral activity. Indeed, from our perspective of teaching as a moral endeavor that occurs in a classroom which itself is conceptualized as a moral context, professional development cannot help but be a moral activity founded on moral reflection and drawing upon, while at the same time continuing to develop, the moral sensibilities described above. Before considering this process, however, we want to look more closely at how teacher professional development involves more than a single aspect of teachers' lives and growth.

In their book on teacher development, Bell and Gilbert (1996) write that "teaching, while supposedly an individual activity, is practiced in a public arena and is a social activity governed by rules and norms, however tightly or loosely defined" (p. 13). They go on to say that, given this view of teaching, "teacher development is also a social activity and may be theorized in terms of social cognition and the social construction of knowledge. Teachers' learning may be seen from a social constructivist perspective" (p. 13). From their perspective, Bell and Gilbert envision teacher development as involving social, personal, and professional development. Bell and Gilbert further argue that effective and lasting change in teaching practices is possible only if teacher development programs are cognizant of each of these aspects of individual development and consciously incorporate activities that address them into such programs. Below, we examine each of the aspects of teacher development as outlined by Bell and Gilbert. Following this, we will elaborate on how professional development in the social, personal, and professional realms draws on the moral sensibilities while at the same time contributing to their development and refinement.

Personal development as part of teacher development involves several actions on the part of teachers. The first concerns recognizing and accepting that part of one's teaching practice requires attention. For some teachers, this may entail acknowledging that "something is broke and needs fixing." For others, it may be part of their practice of continually reflecting upon and assessing their teaching practices. Another part of personal development is attending to the feelings experienced when changes are made in one's teaching practice. For example, changing the way certain activities are conducted, such that children assume more authority and responsibility for their roles in class and over their own learning, can leave some teachers feeling anxious and fearful of losing control of the class (Manke, 1997; Oyler, 1996). Teachers also could feel anxiety when new forms of pedagogy render current kinds of assessment and evaluation meaningless, thus making it difficult for administrators and parents to gauge children's learning. Addressing the feelings experienced when changes are made in deeply held beliefs and practices can be especially difficult when the changes challenge beliefs that are currently held and well-entrenched (Cochran-Smith, 1991). Thus, in attending to these and other feelings that may accompany changes in teaching practices and beliefs about teaching, an important part of personal development is developing a sense of trust in oneself and in the new forms of pedagogy and new understandings of teaching one has acquired. Bell and Gilbert (1996) see personal development leading to teachers feeling more empowered as individuals and as teachers.

Social development as part of teacher development involves developing relationships with colleagues, students, and others that facilitate rethinking and reconstructing what it means to be a teacher. Once again, we see the role of relation in teacher development as making it a moral activity. Developing relations with colleagues as part of teacher development is important in overcoming what many teachers see as the negative aspects of being isolated in separate classrooms. Further, the trust that develops as collaborative relationships with colleagues grow stronger can make possible the sharing of new teaching activities and forms of pedagogy. Different forms of pedagogy may change relationships between teachers and students. As noted above, changes can occur in the way authority is shared in the classroom. Such changes can lead to fundamental shifts in beliefs about teaching, authority, students, and what it means to be a teacher. Bell and Gilbert note that these occur as a result of teachers' interactions with others.

For Bell and Gilbert, the professional aspect of teacher development entails seeing the self as a competent teacher, as a teacher-as-learner, and as a teacher-as-researcher. This vision of the self-as-teacher sets the stage for examining how new teaching practices match new theories and beliefs about teaching. This is not a process of making practices fit with beliefs; rather, it is a careful deliberation of examining how practices and beliefs come together to form new meanings of teaching. Bell and Gilbert note how this occurs as teachers engage in reflection and critical inquiry.

Bell and Gilbert's (1996) view of teacher development is in many ways consistent with our view of teaching as a moral activity. First, Bell and Gilbert say that teaching, "while supposedly an individual activity, is practiced in a public arena and is a social activity governed by rules and norms, however tightly or loosely defined" (p. 13). Our view of teaching as a moral activity flows from the belief that the moral comes into play at those points where the personal or individual and the social intersect. Both views also recognize the important role of rules and norms both in teaching and in understanding the moral dimensions of teaching. Finally, in their view of teacher development, Bell and Gilbert argue that it can be seen as a form of human development. We interpret this as saying that teacher professional development should seek not only to help teachers become better teachers but to also to help them become better people—that is, to become individuals who are more perceptive about recognizing the concerns and needs of others and knowing how to address them. To some this may sound like quite a stretch. However, if one accepts one of the main premises of this book—namely, that teaching is a moral activity because its purpose is to help students become better people (Hansen, 1999), for instance by becoming more knowledgeable and understanding of the world and those that live in it, including themselves—one also must recognize that teacher development, as a moral activity, must involve teachers' efforts to better themselves.

"How Do I Improve My Teaching Practice?"

Whitehead's recognition of the contradictions in his own teaching practice occurred when he watched videotapes of himself teaching. He was able to observe himself holding "two mutually exclusive opposites together in practice" (1993, p. 80). He goes on to say, "I could experience myself holding certain educational values whilst at the same time denying them in my practice" (p. 80). Whitehead based his approach to changing his practice on a dialectic of questions and answers—of asking himself how and why questions, then finding ways to change his practice in the answers. Whitehead's dialectic method proved to be a fruitful approach for him and his students, and we believe some teachers may find this a useful way of examining and changing their teaching practices. Bell and Gilbert's (1996) approach of addressing the social, personal, and professional aspects of oneself as a teacher provides teachers with a means of focusing on the concerns that Whitehead suggests. The opportunity to examine the social, personal, or professional dimensions of their teaching allows teachers to focus more intently on those aspects of their practice that they seek to change. Further, this approach makes it possible for teachers to call on more resources as they work to improve their practice.

As a way of illustrating how teacher development involves the social, personal, and professional aspects of development and is a fundamentally moral activity, we turn to Gore's (1993) examination of her own teaching practices. A student in one of her teacher education courses wrote the following statement in his course journal: "I'm not into this regimented reflective stuff" (Gore, 1993, p. 1). The surprise and dismay Gore felt was the beginning of an examination of her own pedagogy. She saw herself as a radical pedagogue whose teaching practices sought to "oppose oppressive gender, race, class and other social formations, and attempt to facilitate more 'democratic' and 'emancipatory' schooling for all" (1993, p. 5). Upon reading the student's comment, Gore realized that some of her teaching practices were, in Whitehead's terms (1993), negating her beliefs. What Gore perceived in the student's comment was just the type of contradiction Whitehead discussed. The student's comment brought to the foreground inconsistencies in her practice as she worked to implement a radical pedagogy in her teacher education courses. Gore's efforts to locate and understand this inconsistency, as well as others, took her through a careful analysis of feminist and critical pedagogy and their underlying assumptions and implications for teaching practices.

During the examination of her teaching practices, Gore discusses the importance of questioning the fundamental beliefs that underlie our view of teaching and the pedagogies we use. For Gore, this meant questioning the personal beliefs and assumptions she held about teaching and what it means to be a teacher. These beliefs and assumptions must be seen against the social context in which they are played out—that is, the classroom. For Gore, this means that reflection on teaching practices always occurs within the social context of one's teaching and interaction with colleagues. Reflections on teaching practices may lead to changes in the relationships we form with our students as well as how we relate to colleagues. But these relationships are embedded in and influenced by the social contexts in which they occur. This means that as teachers we must acknowledge our position in the "machinery of social/cultural regulation" (Gore, 1993, p. 142)—that is, we should seek to fully understand the nature of the institutions in which we work, be they schools or universities. Unless we engage in some examination of how we and our pedagogy are shaped and influenced by such factors, we may fall prey to implicitly continuing forms of pedagogy we find problematic. Put differently, it is very difficult for any teacher to work completely apart from and uninfluenced by the social and cultural milieu in which she teaches. Finally, changes in our teaching practices and in the ways we develop curricula involve changes in how we conceptualize teaching and the development of theories and beliefs that form the basis for new practices. This is the professional aspect of teacher development that Bell and Gilbert describe. Although brief, this overview of

Gore's efforts to improve her teaching practices illustrates how continuing teacher development involves social, personal, and professional development.

Teacher Development and the Moral Sensibilities

Given this description of teacher development as professional development, and the view of this kind of professional development as a moral activity, how can teachers develop and refine the moral reflection needed for improving teaching practices? Put differently, we ask, how would moral reflection on teaching practices, as professional development, make use of and in turn contribute to the further development of the moral sensibilities? We believe the moral sensibilities are resources that can be called upon in improving practice while at the same time being further developed.

Moral Reflection: We return here to Green's notion of conscience, because we understand reflection, particularly moral reflection, as an act of conscience. As such moral reflection requires us to look deeply and critically at how our teaching practices influence the learning and development of our students. Along with attention to our students' intellectual and moral growth (Hansen, 1999), we are called by conscience to be vigilant to the ways in which the minute-by-minute, day-by-day activities we undertake as teachers continue to influence the type of teachers and people we are becoming. To lose sight of concern either for our students or for ourselves is to lose sight of a commitment that is fundamental to teaching (Fallona, 2000; Hansen, 1998; Sockett, 1993).

Moral reflection provides the basis for the type of professional development we described above. Not only does it provide the foundation for professional development but, as we continue to engage in professional development activities, the ability to reflect on the moral dimensions of our teaching practice becomes more finely tuned. When moral reflection is absent from professional development, it becomes merely a technical exercise, one of adding on more skills or honing the skills we already possess.

Moral Perception: The ability to perceive the needs, concerns, interests, and emotions of our students is crucial if we are to appreciate who they are as individuals and as students. With that said and without being overly obvious, such perception is necessary if we are to be effective teachers to our students. In an earlier chapter we quoted from Bernstein (1975), who said in effect that, if we hope our students will come to understand us as individuals and what we are proposing to teach them, it is first necessary for us to understand *them*. A misperception— that is, a wrong perception, a missed perception, or a failure to perceive at all—of these important aspects of our students leads to a denial of part of their individuality and personhood. In the extremely busy world of the classroom, misperceptions and missed perceptions occur, and it is not our intent to blame teachers for instances where these happen. Rather, we call upon all of us to hone our perceptions so that we can become more finely tuned to our students. Similarly, we must be open to perceiving our own needs, concerns, interests, and emotions as teachers and as individuals. As with our students, to deny these things in ourselves is to deny part of what makes us who we are as people and as teachers. What we learn from our perceptions of our students and of ourselves is the material for continued examinations of the social, personal, and professional dimensions of our development as teachers.

Moral Imagination: It is not possible to engage in the type of professional development described above without moral imagination. Moral imagination plays a crucial role in two ways. First, the very act of committing to professional development marks the realization that change in one's current understandings of teaching practices is possible, necessary, and desirable. Professional development, then, is driven in part by moral imagination, the willingness to see things differently.

Second, professional development as an act of moral imagination is not only the willingness to imagine different kinds of teaching practices but also requires the moral imagination to accomplish the changes in practice. In other words, professional development demands the ability to carefully examine current practices in a way that recognizes areas of potential change. As noted earlier in this chapter, this involves a critique of present practices as well as reflection upon the social, personal, and professional dimensions of one's teaching practice. At the same time, though, professional development involves being cognizant of a realm of potential possibilities for change.

An example might better illustrate these points. Several years ago I (Cary) came to the realization that my teaching practices were neither what I wanted them to be nor what I hoped they could be. My own reflections and assessments as well as evaluations from students indicated areas in need of change. As I read over the students' evaluations and reflected on the course, I had some ideas of how I wanted to teach the course differently. I wanted the students to be more engaged in discussion, I wanted to ask more insightful questions that challenged students' views yet would not intimidate them. I imagined a more exciting class in which we would all be engaged in examining teaching practices and curricula that would best meet our future and present students' needs. I sought out the teaching consultants at my university. As I talked with them I outlined the type of teaching I had in mind. Together we worked out a plan that involved some observations of my class along with focus groups with students and some individual meetings with me. As this process moved along, I came to see that it encompassed not just what I did in class with my students but how I thought about myself as a teacher, the role I wanted to play in the classroom, and my vision of what teacher education should be. In short, this process involved changes in the social, personal, and professional aspects of my practice. Over the course of the next few semesters, I implemented a number of changes; some were very successful, some I'm still working to refine. As I refine them, I continue to imagine what I hope will happen with my students in my courses. I have become a better teacher and in turn developed my moral imagination. Although brief and personal, I think this example highlights how professional development draws upon but also contributes to the development of moral imagination.

Moral Courage: To continue with this example, I would be remiss if I did not elaborate on how I felt during this entire process. It was not difficult for me to admit that some changes in my teaching practices were needed. Nor was it difficult for me to see that they would be desirable. The data telling me about the need and desirability of change were in my hand. I was disappointed to read them, but they presented an accurate picture of what was happening and not happening in my course. What took courage was admitting that I was not the teacher I thought I was. My image of myself as a teacher, my vision of what teaching and teacher education ought to be, and the way I went about teaching were not what the students were experiencing (Whitehead, 1993). In other words, what I imagined and what was occurring were two different things. I had to face up to the fact that there was quite a mismatch between the two. In Bell and Gilbert's view (1996), I felt this realization in the personal dimension of my teaching. This took courage to accept, as did seeking assistance from colleagues. I felt as though I had laid bare my inadequacies in front of colleagues who could not only do better but knew better. These were the folks who were going to observe me in my classroom. I told my students that someone would be coming to observe me and that it was part of the reflective teaching we had been talking about. In other words, I presented it as a way of modeling for them one aspect of reflective practice. Although the observations went well, and I did not feel nearly as nervous as I thought I would, it was nonetheless a slightly uncomfortable experience. After the observations, I met with the teaching consultant who had observed me. I felt a bit apprehensive during each of our meetings, but I learned quite a lot from the discussions. I felt I needed a bit of courage each time I met with the consultant. In the end, though, I felt I was a better teacher—and subsequent evaluations and reflections seemed to verify my feelings.

One purpose of recounting my professional development experience is to personalize what it is we are saying. But that is not the only reason. It certainly is not to hold myself up as the quintessential example of professional development. Rather, we believe it highlights a key point we made in the section on moral courage earlier in this chapter. That point is that there we offered, and still advocate for, a prosaic definition of moral courage. The very act of engaging in authentic professional development that seeks to make real changes in beliefs and practices calls for moral courage. At the same time, our participation in professional development contributes back to our store, if you will, of moral courage. We acknowledge and are thankful that there will always be exemplary teachers of great moral courage, for they inspire us. But we are also thankful for teachers and colleagues, much less well known but equally courageous, who join us in the moral work of professional development.

CONCLUSION

We recently discovered in conversation that a particular cultural image from our childhood had acquired a special meaning in relation to the moral dimensions of teaching. In the 1960s television variety shows (for Cary, it was *The Ed Sullivan Show* in the United States; for Bill, *Opportunity Knocks* in Britain), there sometimes were acts that entailed a single performer keeping a number of plates spinning atop what looked like wooden sticks. The sticks, of which there were many (perhaps twenty or thirty), were attached to long wooden beams on the floor, so they extended to about three and a half or four feet high. The performer would begin spinning the first plate on the first stick. He or she would proceed to the second plate on the second stick and so on, until each stick was topped with a spinning plate. When the fourth or fifth plate was set in motion, it would be necessary to run back to the first and second ones to give them another spin to keep them going. The goal was to have all the plates spinning at the same time and to avoid having any fall off and break.

Cary writes:

> This image often came to my mind during my early years as a teacher when I would reflect after a particularly busy day teaching young children. I felt like this performer as I would repeatedly check in with each of the twenty or so children in my care to see if each was settling into the classroom that day, or engaged in an interesting activity, or getting along well with peers, or feeling okay about just hanging out. My goal and hope was to just keep all the plates spinning—to keep all the children safe, engaged in good and interesting activities, and happy. Like many beginning teachers (and experienced teachers as well), I felt I did not have the time to examine what it was that kept the plates spinning, or slowed them down, or even if keeping them spinning was a good idea. As I developed the ability to reflect upon my practice, I began to see that such brief encounters, which some days seem to be all that happened (I confess that I still have days like this), were times of moral contact between me and my students, whether they were four-year-olds or juniors in college.

A fundamental part of our message in this book is that teachers *do* have a moral sense. They inherently know that teaching is a moral activity. What we have suggested here are ways of affirming and nurturing that awareness. As we come to the end of the book, we hope we have made this clear. We believe our view of teaching as moral contact presents us with a richer view of our work as teachers. Throughout this book we have looked below the surface of teaching, to peer deeply into its moral dimensions. Like watching the performer trying to keep the plates spinning, we hope our descriptions and examples of teaching have honored the complex, ambiguous, and demanding work of teaching. But, unlike the performer— who seemed unaware of the invisible principles of physics that made it possible to keep the plates spinning and also of the very purpose or value of the act—we have revealed both the moral foundations of classroom events and the moral purposiveness of teaching.

Above all, our message in this book is as follows. Teaching is inherently, unavoidably, and primarily moral action and interaction: that is, moral contact. This is the case whatever kind of teacher you are and whatever context you work in. Furthermore, the moral dimensions of teaching are usually hard to see: They do not immediately leap out at you, but need to be carefully traced in the myriad small and seemingly insignificant events and acts that make up classroom interaction. However, it is both possible and desirable for teachers to become attuned to the moral meanings that are expressed and negotiated in their classrooms. The moral sensibilities are available to any teacher who wants to gain a deeper understanding of interaction in her own classroom. We also wish to add that, in our opinion, teachers themselves are much better placed than outsider observers to grasp the moral subtleties, complexities, and ambiguities of this interaction, since no one has a richer knowledge of the contextual features of a classroom than the teacher who works there. Finding the moral in classroom interaction is not easy. But we can attest from our own experience that, once a teacher becomes fully aware of this dimension of classroom life and perceives its richness and its significance, the classroom, and especially those who spend time in it day after day, will never look the same again.

REFERENCES

Amirault, C. (1995). The good teacher, the good student: Identifications of a student teacher. In J. Gallop (Ed.), *Pedagogy: The question of impersonation* (pp. 64–78). Bloomington: Indiana University Press.

Apple, M. (1982). *Education and power*. Boston: Routledge & Kegan Paul.

Atkinson, D. (1999). TESOL and culture. *TESOL Quarterly, 33*, 625–654.

Atkinson, J., & Heritage, J. (Eds.). (1984). *Structures of social action*. Cambridge: Cambridge University Press.

Ayers, W. (1993). *To teach*. New York: Teachers College Press.

Ayers, W. (1998). Teaching as an ethical enterprise. *The Educational Forum, 63* (Fall) 52–57.

Ayers, W., & Ford, P. (Eds.). (1996). *City kids, city teachers: Reports from the front row*. New York: New Press.

Ayers, W., Hunt, J. A., & Quinn, T. (Eds.). (1998). *Teaching for social justice: A democracy and education reader*. New York: Teachers College Press.

Baerwald, T. J., & Fraser, C. (1995). *World geography: A global perspective*. Needham, MA: Prentice Hall.

Bakhtin, M. M. (1981). The dialogic imagination (C. Emerson & M. Holquist, Trans.). Austin: University of Texas Press.

Ball, S. J. (Ed.). (1990). *Foucault and education. Disciplines and knowledge*. London: Routledge.

Ballenger, C. (1997). Social identities, moral narratives, scientific argumentation: Science talk in a bilingual classroom. *Language and Education, 13*, 1–14.

Banks, J. A., Beyer, B. K., Contreras, G., Crave, J., Ladson-Billings, G., McFarland, M. A., & Parker, W. C. (1995). *The world around us*. New York: Macmillan/McGraw-Hill.

Barber, B. R. (1995). *Jihad vs. McWorld*. New York: Times Books.

Barnes, D., Britton, J., & Rosen, H. (1969). *Language, the learner, and the school*. Harmondworth, UK: Penguin.

Bauman, Z. (1993). *Postmodern ethics*. Cambridge, MA: Blackwell.

Bauman, Z. (1995). *Life in fragments: Essays in postmodern morality*. Oxford: Blackwell.

Bauman, Z. (1997). *Postmodernity and its discontents*. New York: New York University Press.

Beane, J. (1997). *Curriculum integration: Designing the core of democratic education*. New York: Teachers College Press.

Bell, B., & Gilbert, J. (1996*). Teacher development: A model from science education*. London: Falmer Press.

Bernstein, B. (1975). *Toward a theory of educational transmissions: Vol. 3. Class, codes and control*. London: Routledge & Kegan Paul.

Bernstein, B. (1990). *The structuring of pedagogic discourse: Vol. 4. Class, codes, and control*. London: Routledge.

Bernstein, B. (1996). *Pedagogy, symbolic control and ideology: Theory, research, critique*. Bristol, PA: Taylor & Francis.

Beyer, L. (1991). Schooling, moral commitment and the preparation of teachers. *Journal of Teacher Education, 42*, 205–215.

Beyer, L. (Ed.). (1996). *Creating democratic classrooms: The struggle to integrate*. New York: Teachers College Press.

Bhabha, H. K. (1994). *The location of culture*. London: Routledge.

Block, A. A. (1997). *I'm only bleeding: Education as the practice of social violence against children*. New York: Peter Lang.

Boehm, R. G. (1997). *World geography: A physical and cultural approach*. New York: Glencoe/ McGraw-Hill.

Boehm, R. G., Armstrong, D. G., & Hunkins, F. P. (1996). *Geography: The world and its people*. New York: Glencoe/McGraw-Hill.

Boostrom, R. (1991). The nature and functions of classroom rules. *Curriculum Inquiry, 21*, 193–216.

Bourdieu, P. (1971). Intellectual field and creative project. In M. F. D. Young (Ed.), *Knowledge and control: New directions for the sociology of education* (pp. 161–188). London: Collier-MacMillan.

Bourdieu, P. (1991) *Language and symbolic power* (G. Raymond & M. Adamson, Trans.). Cambridge, MA: Harvard University Press.

Bowers, C.A. (1984). *The promise of theory: Education and the politics of cultural change*. New York: Teachers College Press.

Bowers, C.A. (1995). *Educating for an ecologically sustainable culture: Rethinking moral education, creativity, intelligence and other modern orthodoxies*. Albany, NY: SUNY Press.

Brantlinger, E. (1993). *The politics of social class in secondary school*. New York: Teachers College Press.

Bruner, J. S. (1986). *Actual minds, possible worlds*. Cambridge, MA: Harvard University Press.

Burbules, N. (1993). *Dialogue in teaching: Theory and practice*. New York: Teachers College Press.

Burbules, N. (1997). Teaching and the tragic sense of education. In N. Burbules & D. Hansen (Eds.), *Teaching and its predicaments* (pp. 65–77). Boulder, CO: Westview Press.

Burbules, N., & Hansen, D. (Eds.). (1997). *Teaching and its predicaments*. Boulder, CO: Westview Press.

Buzzelli, C. A. (1995). Teacher–child discourse in the early childhood classroom: A dialogic model of self-regulation and moral development. In S. Reifel (Ed.), *Advances in early education and day care* (pp. 271–294). Greenwich, CT: JAI Press.

Buzzelli, C. A. (1996). The moral implications of teacher–child discourse in early childhood classrooms. *Early Childhood Research Quarterly, 11,* 515–534.

Cazden, C. (1986). Classroom discourse. In M. D. Wittrock (Ed.), *Handbook of research on teaching* (3rd ed. pp. 432–463). New York: Macmillan.

Cazden, C. (1988). *Classroom discourse: The language of teaching and learning.* Portsmouth, NH: Heinemann.

Chang, K. A. (1996). Culture, power and the social construction of morality: Moral voices of Chinese students. *Journal of Moral Education, 25,* 141–157.

Cisneros, S. (1989). *The house on Mango Street.* New York: Vintage.

Clandinin, D. J., & Connelly, F. M. (1995). *Teachers' professional knowledge landscapes.* New York: Teachers College Press.

Cochran-Smith, M. (1991). Learning to teach against the grain. *Harvard Educational Review, 61,* 279–310.

Coles, R. (1989). *The call of stories; Teaching and the moral imagination.* Boston: Houghton Mifflin.

Connelly, F. M., & Clandinin, D. J. (Eds.). (1999). *Shaping a professional identity: Stories of educational practice.* New York: Teachers College Press.

Cummins, J. (1980). The cross-lingual dimensions of language proficiency: Implications for bilingual education and the optimal age issue. *TESOL Quarterly, 14,* 175–188.

Darling-Hammond, L., Wise, A., & Klein, S. (Eds.). (1995). *A license to teach: Building a profession for 21st-century schools.* Boulder, CO: Westview Press.

Davey, A. (1983). *Learning to be prejudiced: Growing up in multi-ethnic Britain.* London: Edward Arnold.

Davies, B., & Hunt, R. (1994). Classroom competencies and marginal positionings. *British Journal of Sociology of Education, 15,* 389–409.

Davis, K. A. & Golden, J. M. (1994). Teacher culture and children's voices in an urban kindergarten center. *Linguistics and Education, 6,* 261–287.

Delpit, L. (1988). The silenced dialogue: Power and pedagogy in educating other people's children. *Harvard Educational Review, 58,* 280–298.

Denzin, N. (1992). *Symbolic interactionism and cultural studies.* London: Blackwell.

Dewey, J. (1909/1975). *Moral principles in education.* Carbondale: Southern Illinois University Press.

Dewey, J. (1938). *Experience and education.* New York: Macmillan.

Dewey, J., & Tufts, J. H. (1936). *Ethics.* New York: Henry Holt.

Dilg, M. (1999). *Race and culture in the classroom: Teaching and learning through multicultural education.* New York: Teachers College Press.

Dillon, J. T. (1994). *Using discussion in classrooms.* Buckingham,UK: Open University Press.

Du Bois, W. E. B. (1903/1989). *The souls of black folk.* New York: Penguin.

Duff, P. A., & Uchida, Y. (1997). The negotiation of teachers' sociocultural identities and practices in postsecondary EFL classrooms. *TESOL Quarterly, 31,* 451–486.

Edwards, D., & Mercer, N. (1987). *Common knowledge: The development of understanding in the classroom.* New York: Routledge.

Eggins, S. (1994). *An introduction to systemic functional linguistics.* London: Printer.

Ellsworth, M. (1989). Why doesn't this feel empowering? Working through the repressive myths of critical pedagogy. *Harvard Educational Review, 59,* 297–324.

Ellsworth, E. (1997). *Teaching positions.* New York: Teachers College Press.

Fairclough, N. (1989). *Language and power.* London: Longman.

Fallona, C. (2000). Manner in teaching: A study in observing and interpreting teachers' moral values. *Teaching and Teacher Education, 16,* 681–695.

Fenstermacher, G. D. (1992). The concepts of method and manner in teaching. In F. Oser & J. L. Patry (Eds.), *Effective and responsible teaching* (pp. 95–108). San Francisco: Jossey-Bass.

Fenstermacher, G. D. (1999, April). *Method, style, and manner in classroom teaching.* Paper presented at the annual meeting of the American Educational Research Association, Montreal, Quebec.

Foley, D. E. (1996). The silent Indian as cultural production. In B. A. Levinson, D. E. Foley, & D. C. Holland (Eds.), *The cultural production of the educated person* (pp. 79–91). Albany, NY: SUNY Press.

Foucault, M. (1977). *Discipline and punish* (A. M. Sheridan Smith, Trans.). New York: Pantheon.

Foucault, M. (1980). *Power/knowledge. Selected interviews and other writings of Michel Foucault* (C. Gordon, Ed.). Brighton, UK: Harvester.

Freire, P. (1972). *Pedagogy of the oppressed* (M. B. Ramos, Trans.). London: Penguin.

Gallas, K. (1995). *How children talk their way into science.* New York: Teachers College Press.

Gallas, K. (1998). *"Sometimes I can be anything." Power, gender, and identity in a primary classroom.* New York: Teachers College Press.

García, E. (1999). *Student cultural diversity: Understanding and meeting the challenge.* Boston: Houghton Mifflin.

Gee, J. P. (1992). *The social mind: Language, ideology and social practice.* New York: Bergin & Garvey.

Gee, J. P. (1996). *Social linguistics and literacies.* Bristol, PA: Taylor & Francis.

Gergen, K. J. (1991). *The saturated self: Dilemmas of identity in contemporary life.* New York: Basic Books.

Gibbons, P. (1998). Classroom talk and the learning of new registers in a second language. *Language and Education, 12,* 99–118.

Giroux, H. A. (1988). *Teachers as intellectuals: Towards a critical pedagogy of learning.* Granby, MA: Bergin & Garvey.

Goethals, M. S., & Howard, R. (2000). *Student teaching: A process approach to reflective practice: A guide for student, intern, and beginning teachers.* Upper Saddle River, NJ: Merrill.

Goodlad, J. I. (1990). *Teachers for our nation's schools.* San Francisco: Jossey-Bass.

Goodlad, J. I. (1994). *Educational renewal: Better teachers, better schools.* San Francisco: Jossey-Bass.

Goodman, J. (1992). *Elementary schooling for critical democracy.* Albany, NY: SUNY Press.

Gore, J. (1993). *The struggle for pedagogies: Critical and feminist discourses as regimes of truth.* New York: Routledge.

Gore, J. M. (1994, April). *Power and pedagogy: An empirical investigation of four sites.* Paper presented at the Annual Meeting of the American Educational Research Association, New Orleans, LA.

Gore, J. M. (1996, November). *Understanding power relations in pedagogy.* Paper presented at the joint meeting of the Australian Association for Research in Education and the Educational Research Association, Singapore.

Green, T. F. (1984). *The formation of conscience in an age of technology.* Syracuse, NY: Syracuse University, the John Dewey Society.

Green, T. F. (1999). *Voices: The educational formation of the conscience.* Notre Dame, IN: University of Notre Dame Press.

Grudgeon, E., & Woods, P. (1990). *Educating all: Multicultural perspectives in the primary school.* London: Routledge.

Gumperz, J. (1982). *Discourse strategies.* Cambridge, UK: Cambridge University Press.

Gumperz, J., & Hymes, D. (Eds.). (1982). *Directions in sociolinguistics: The ethnography of speaking.* New York: Holt, Rinehart & Winston.

Habermas, J. (1984). *Theory of communicative action, Vol 1.* London: Heinemann.

Halliday, M. A. K. (1978). *Language as a social semiotic: The social interpretation of language and meaning.* London: Edward Arnold.

Halliday, M. A. K. (1993). Towards a language-based theory of learning. *Linguistics and Education, 5,* 93–116.

Halliday, M. A. K., & Hasan, R. (1989). *Language, context and text: Aspects of language in a social-semiotic perspective.* Oxford: Oxford University Press.

Hansen, D. T. (1998). The moral is in the practice. *Teaching and Teacher Education. 14,* 643–655.

Hansen, D. T. (1999). Understanding students. *Journal of Curriculum and Supervision, 14,* 171–185.

Hargreaves, A. & Fullan, M. G. (1992). Introduction. In A. Hargreaves & M. G. Fullan (Eds.), *Understanding teacher development* (pp.1–19). London: Cassell.

Harklau, L. (1999). Representing culture in the ESL writing classroom. In E. Hinkel (Ed.), *Culture in second language teaching and learning* (pp. 109–130). Cambridge, UK: Cambridge University Press.

Harklau, L. (2000). From the "good kids" to the "worst": Representations of English language learners across educational settings. *TESOL Quarterly, 34*, 35–67.

Harre, R., & Van Langenhove, L. (Eds.). (1999). *Positioning theory: Moral contexts of intentional action.* Malden, MA: Blackwell.

Hatcher, R., & Troyna, B. (1993). Racialization and children. In C. McCarthy & W. Crichlow (Eds.), *Race, identity, and representation in education* (pp. 109–125). New York: Routledge.

Heath, S. B. (1983). *Ways with words: Language, life, and work in communities and classrooms.* Cambridge, UK: Cambridge University Press.

Holland, D., Lachicotte, W., Skinner, D., & Cain, C. (1998). *Identity and agency in cultural worlds.* Cambridge, MA: Harvard University Press.

Hoskin, K. (1990). Foucault under examination: The crypto-educationalist unmasked. In S. J. Ball (Ed.), *Foucault and education. Disciplines and knowledge* (pp. 29–53). London: Routledge.

Jackson, P. W., Boostrom, R. E., & Hansen, D. T. (1993). *The moral life of schools.* San Francisco: Jossey-Bass.

Janangelo, J. (1993). To serve, with love: Liberation theory and the mystification of teaching. In P. Kahaney, L. A. M. Perry, & J. Janangelo (Eds.), *Theoretical and critical perspectives on teacher change* (pp. 134–150). Norwood, NJ: Ablex.

Johnston, B., & Buzzelli, C. (in press). Expressive morality in a collaborative learning activity: A case study in the creation of moral meaning. *Language and Education.*

Johnston, B., Juhász, A., Marken, J., & Ruiz, B. R. (1998). The ESL teacher as moral agent. *Research in the Teaching of English, 32*, 161–181.

Johnston, D. K. (1991). Cheating: Reflections on a moral dilemma. *Journal of Moral Education, 20*, 283–291.

Kenner, C. (1999). Children's understandings of text in a multilingual nursery. *Language and Education, 13*, 1–16.

Koppich, J. (2000). *Studies of excellence in teacher education: Preparation in a five-year program.* Washington, DC: AACTE Publications.

Lakoff, G. (1987) *Women, fire, and dangerous things.* Chicago: University of Chicago Press.

Lakoff, G., & Johnson, M. (1980) *Metaphors we live by.* Chicago: University of Chicago Press.

Larmore, C. (1987). *Patterns of moral complexity.* New York: Cambridge University Press.

Lather, P. (1991). *Getting smart: Feminist research and pedagogy with/in the postmodern.* London: Routledge.

Lather, P. (1992). Postmodernity and the human sciences. In S. Kvale (Ed.), *Psychology and postmodernism* (pp. 88–109). London: Sage.

Lave, J., & Chailkin, S. (1993). *Understanding practice: Perspectives on activity and context.* New York: Cambridge University Press.

Lemke, J. (1990). *Talking science: Language, learning and values*. Norwood, NJ: Ablex.

Lotman, Y. M. (1988). Text within a text. *Soviet Psychology, 26,* 3, 32–51.

Luke, A. (1988). *Literacy, textbooks, and ideology*. London: Falmer.

Lutz, C. A., & Collins, J. L. (1993). *Reading National Geographic*. Chicago: University of Chicago Press.

MacCannell, D. (1992). *Empty meeting grounds: The tourist papers*. London: Routledge.

Macedo, D. (1994). *Literacies of power*. Boulder, CO: Westview.

MacLure, M. (1993). Arguing for your self: Identity as an organizing principle in teachers' jobs and lives. *British Educational Research Journal, 19,* 311–322.

Manke, M. (1997). *Classroom power relations: Understanding student–teacher interaction*. Mahwah, NJ: Lawrence Erlbaum.

Martin-Jones, M., & Saxena, M. (1996). Turn-taking, power asymmetries, and the positioning of bilingual participants in classroom discourse. *Linguistics and Education, 8,* 105– 123.

Maxwell, M. (1991). *Moral inertia: Ideas for social action*. Niwot: University Press of Colorado.

McCadden, B. M. (1998). *It's hard to be good: Moral complexity, construction, and connection in a kindergarten classroom*. New York: Peter Lang.

McCarthy, C., & Crichlow, W. (Eds.). (1993). *Race, identity, and representation in education*. New York: Routledge.

McElroy-Johnson, B. (1993) Giving voice to the voiceless. *Harvard Educational Review, 63,* 85–104.

McKay, S. L., & Wong, S.-L. C. (1996). Multiple discourses, multiple identities: Investment and agency in second-language learning among Chinese adolescent immigrant students. *Harvard Educational Review, 66,* 577–608.

McLaren, P. (1989). *Life in schools: An introduction to critical pedagogy in the foundations of education*. New York: Longman.

Mehan, H. (1979). *Learning lessons: Social organization in the classroom*. Cambridge, MA: Harvard University Press.

Michaels, S. (1981). "Sharing time": Children's narrative styles and differential access to literacy. *Language in Society, 10,* 423–442.

Michaels, S. (1991). The dismantling of narrative. In A. McCabe & C. Peterson (Eds.), *Developing narrative structure* (pp. 303–351). Hillsdale, NJ: Lawrence Erlbaum.

Milton, O., Pollio, H. R., & Eison, J. A. (1986). *Making sense of college grades*. San Francisco: Jossey-Bass.

Noblit, G. W. & Dempsey, V. O. (1996). *The social construction of virtue: The moral life of schools*. Albany, NY: SUNY Press.

Noddings, N. (1984). *Caring: A feminine approach to ethics and moral education*. Berkeley: University of California Press.

Noddings, N. (1992). *The challenge to care in schools*. New York: Teachers College Press.

Nyberg, D., & Farber, P. (1986). Authority in education. *Teachers College Record, 88,* 4–14.

O'Connor, M. C., & Michaels, S. (1993). Aligning academic task and participation status through revoicing: Analysis of a classroom discourse strategy. *Anthropology and Education, 24,* 318–335.

O'Connor, M. C., & Michaels, S. (1996). Shifting participant frameworks: Orchestrating thinking practices in group discussion. In D. Hicks (Ed.), *Discourse, learning, and schooling* (pp. 63–103). New York: Cambridge University Press.

Olsen, L. (1988). *Crossing the schoolhouse border: Immigrant students and the California public schools.* San Francisco: California Tomorrow.

Otte, G. (1995). In-Voicing: Beyond the voice debate. In J. Gallop (Ed.), *Pedagogy: The question of impersonation* (pp. 147–154). Bloomington: Indiana University Press.

Ovando, C. J., & McLaren, P. (Eds.). (2000). *The politics of multiculturalism and bilingual education: Students and teachers caught in the crossfire.* Boston: McGraw-Hill.

Oyler, C. (1996). *Making room for students: Sharing teacher authority in room 104.* New York: Teachers College Press.

Pagano, J. A. (1991). Relating to one's students: Identity, morality, stories, and questions. *Journal of Moral Education, 20,* 257–266.

Peirce, B. N. (1995). Social identity, investment, and language learning. *TESOL Quarterly, 29,* 9–31.

Peters, R. S. (1966). *Ethics and education.* London: Allen & Unwin.

Philips, S. (1983). *The invisible culture: Communication in classroom and community in the Warm Springs Indian Reservation.* New York: Longman.

Placier, M. (1996). An action research approach to a contradiction in teaching: Reconciling grades with democratic education. *Action in Teacher Education, 18(3),* 23–32.

Plowden Report. (1967). *Children and their schools.* Report of the Central Advisory Council of Education (England). London: HMSO.

Rice, S., & Burbules, N. C. (1993). Communicative virtues and educational relations. In H. Alexander (Ed.), *Philosophy of education 1992: Proceedings of the forty-eighth annual meeting of the Philosophy of Education Society* (pp. 34–44). Normal, IL: Philosophy of Education Society.

Richardson, V. (Ed.). (1997). *Constructivist teacher education: Building new understandings.* London: Falmer Press.

Rivage-Seul, M. K. (1987). Peace education: Moral imagination and the pedagogy of the oppressed. *Harvard Educational Review, 57,* 153–169.

Rogoff, B. (1989). *Apprenticeship in thinking: Cognitive development in social context.* New York: Oxford University Press.

Rong, X. L., & Preissle, J. (1998). *Educating immigrant students. What we need to know to meet the challenges.* Thousand Oaks, CA: Corwin.

Said, E. W. (1994). *Representations of the intellectual.* New York: Pantheon.

Sarup, M. (1996). *Identity, culture, and the postmodern world.* Athens: University of Georgia Press.

Sennett, R. (1980). *Authority.* New York: Knopf.

Shannon, S. M. (1995). The hegemony of English: A case study of one bilingual classroom as a site of resistance. *Linguistics and Education, 7*, 175–200.

Simpson, P., & Garrison, J. (1995). Teaching and moral perception. *Teachers College Record, 97*, 252–278.

Sockett, H. (1993). *The moral base of teacher professionalism.* New York: Teachers College Press.

Spindler, G. (Ed.). (1982). *Doing ethnography of schooling: Educational anthropology in action.* New York: Holt, Rinehart & Winston.

Strauss, C., & Quinn, N. (1997). *A cognitive theory of cultural meaning.* Cambridge, UK: Cambridge University Press.

Stubbs, M., & Robinson, B. (1979). Analyzing classroom language. In V. J. Lee (Ed.), *Language development: A reader.* New York: Open University Press.

Tannen, D. (1989). *Talking voices: Repetition, dialogue, and imagery in conversational discourse.* New York: Cambridge University Press.

Tobin, J. J. (2000). *"Good guys don't wear hats": Children's talk about the media.* New York: Teachers College Press.

Tom, A. (1984). *Teaching as a moral craft.* New York: Longman.

Valli, L. (1990). Moral approaches to reflective practice. In R. T. Clift, W. R. Houston, & M. C. Pugach (Eds.), *Encouraging reflective practice in education* (pp. 39–56). New York: Teachers College Press.

van Dijk, T. A. (Ed.). (1985). *Handbook of discourse analysis (4 vol.).* London: Academic Press.

van Dijk, T. A. (Ed.). (1997). *Discourse studies: A multidisciplinary introduction.* London: Sage Publications.

Vygotsky, L. S. (1978). *Mind in society.* Cambridge, MA: Harvard University Press.

Wells, G. (1992). The centrality of talk in education. In K. Norman (Ed.), *Thinking voices: The work of the National Oracy Project* (pp. 283–310). London: Houghton & Stoughton.

Wells, G. (1993). Re-evaluating the IRF sequence: A proposal for the articulation of theories of activity and discourse for the analysis of teaching and learning in the classroom. *Linguistics and Education, 5*, 1–37.

Wells, G. (1997, March). *Modes of meaning-making in a science activity.* Paper presented at the meeting of the American Educational Research Association, Chicago.

Wells, G. (1999). *Dialogic inquiry: Towards a sociocultural practice and theory of education.* New York: Cambridge University Press.

Wertsch, J. (1991). *Voices of the mind: A sociocultural approach to mediated action.* Cambridge, MA: Harvard University Press.

Whitehead, J. (1993). *The growth of educational knowledge. Creating your own living educational theories.* Bournemouth, UK: Hyde.

Wilder, L. I. (1935/1981). *Little house on the prairie.* New York: HarperCollins.

Willett, J. (1995). Becoming first graders in an L2: An ethnographic study of L2 socialization. *TESOL Quarterly, 29*, 473–503.

Wood, D., Bruner, J., & Ross, G. (1976). The role of tutoring in problem solving. *Journal of Child Psychology and Psychiatry, 17,* 89–100.

Young, M. F. D. (Ed.). (1971). *Knowledge and control. New directions for the sociology of education.* London: Collier-Macmillan.

Young, R. (1984). Teaching equals indoctrination: The dominant epistemic practices of our schools. *British Journal of Educational Studies, 32,* 220–238.

Young, R. (1988). Critical teaching and learning. *Educational Theory, 38,* 47–59.

Young, R. (1990). *Toward a critical theory of education.* New York: Teachers College Press.

Young, R. (1992). *Critical theory and classroom talk.* Clevedon, UK: Multilingual Matters.

Zeichner, K. (2000). *Studies of excellence in teacher education: Preparation in the undergraduate years.* Washington, DC: AACTE Publications.

Zeichner, K., Melnick, S., & Gomez, M. (Eds.). (1996). *Currents of reform in preservice teacher education.* New York: Teachers College Press.

INDEX

teacher development, 146–48
 aimed at improving students'
  learning, 144
 based on examination of one's
  own practices, 145, 149, 150
 use of moral reflection in, 151
 with moral courage, 154–55
 with moral imagination,
  152–53
 see also teacher education
teacher education, 17, 119, 125,
  143
 examination of personal philosophy, 137
 field experience, 140, 141
 methods and subject matter
  courses, 138–40
 redefinition of teacher student
  relationship, 133–36
 see also moral sensibilities
teachers
 complexities experienced by, 5,
  10
 dual authority of, 56–59, 63, 71
 moral agency of, 3, 7, 8–9,
  51–52, 54, 118, 120
 in judgments about what and
  how to teach, 12–13
 in mediating curricular materials, 105

moral commitment necessitated
  by, 14
 in responding to various cultural values, 116
 opportunities to learn from
  experience, 11–12
 role of, shown in discourse, 38
 see also teacher development;
  teaching
teaching
 complexity of, 2, 10, 118,
  129–30
 limitations of, 11–12
 relational nature of, 8–9, 73, 93,
  104–105, 119–20
 complexity of multiple identities in, 114–15
 cultural misunderstanding an
  obstacle to, 90–91
 social negotiation in, 121–22

Wells, G., 28
Whitehead, 61, 144–45
Willett, J., 108

Young, 31–32